Cooking with Tea

Techniques and Recipes
for Appetizers,
Entrées, Desserts,
and More

Robert Wemischner and Diana Rosen

photography by Susan Bourgoin

Cooking *with* Tea

Techniques and Recipes
for Appetizers,
Entrées, Desserts,
and More

Periplus Editions
Boston • Rutland, VT • Singapore

First published in 2000 by Periplus Editions (HK) Ltd.,
with editorial offices at 153 Milk Street, Boston,
Massachusetts 02109
and 5 Little Road #08-01, Singapore 536983.

Library of Congress Card Number: 00-103437

ISBN:962-593-816-8

Distributed by

USA
Tuttle Publishing
Distribution Center
Airport Industrial Park
364 Innovation Drive
North Clarendon, VT 05759-9436
Tel: (802) 773-8930
Tel: (800) 526-2778

Japan
Tuttle Shuppan
RK Building, 2nd Floor
2-13-10 Shimo-Meguro, Meguro-Ku
Tokyo 153 0064
Tel: (03) 5437-0171
Fax: (03) 5437-0755

Canada
Raincoast Books
8680 Cambie Street
Vancouver, British Columbia
V6P 6M9
Tel: (604) 323-7100
Fax: (604) 323-2600

Southeast Asia
Berkeley Books Pte Ltd
5 Little Road #08-01
Singapore 536983
Tel: (65) 280-1330
Fax: (65) 280-6290

05 04 03 02 01 00   1 2 3 4 5 6 7 8 9 10

Design by Jeannet Leendertse

To all the visionaries
in the wonderful world of teadom
who have inspired and encouraged us
to take tea to another dimension.

Contents

part three

Appendices   123

Acknowledgments

Many thanks to Susan Bourgoin for her vivid, elegant styling and photographic skills and to her husband Ken Bourgoin; Ms. Sandy Sado and Mr. Kittibhoom Harnpatanakitpanich for critical support duties in the kitchen. To Devan Shah of Chado Tea Room, Los Angeles and India Tea Importers, Montebello, California, many many thanks for the generous use of the teas used in our recipes. Thanks to Dan Robertson of The Tea House, Naperville, Illinois, for perspective and specific ideas on classic Chinese tea recipes. And thanks to Ken Rudee and Cheryl Valk of Barnes & Watson, Seattle, for teas and support of our vision that cooking with tea is here to stay.

From Diana, thanks to my family and friends for support above and beyond, especially to Patti and Joe Anastasi, Manette Rosen and Joel Bender, and Dona Schweiger. From Robert, thanks to my wife, Leslie, and our children, Lauren and Chad, for patience and for eating just one more version.

part one

Tea Basics

An Introduction

As lovers of the leaf, we have come to believe tea holds a spell of magic that provides comfort, serenity, peace. It is this very magic that inspired us to take the leap from being enthusiasts of tea as a magnificent drink to aficionados of tea as a vibrant, innovative, and extremely versatile ingredient in cooking.

We began, as most tea lovers do, by sampling. Then, the passion took hold, and we found ourselves sleuthing out the best, rarest, most incredible tasting tea of the season. Unlike wine, tea cannot be "put down" for future drinking; its pleasure is of the moment, and what a moment it can be when you discover a tea that captures your mind and your palate.

Was it a Lu'an Melon, a barely processed green tea from China with a silky, peachy-melon taste, or the inimitable fragrance and full mouth feel of the highest grade Ti Kwan Yin oolong made fresh just last week in Taiwan? Maybe it was the delicate, almost-there quality of the finest white tea, a Silver Needle perhaps, floating downward in a glass tumbler, a sylph naiad in water. Savoring the sweet green freshness of a just-picked Dragonwell is like sipping a heavenly nectar. Warming yourself by the fire with a hearty, winey Keemun is one of life's simplest luxuries. Cooling off with the classic American style of tea, iced, is one of the thousand pleasures of this world's favorite beverage. The list goes on and on.

This passion for tea is not just our story, for it began thousands of years ago when Buddhist monks brought tea seeds from China—the birthplace of tea—to Japan, Korea, India, and other Asian countries that continue to grow tea today, on and off the land of monasteries.

WHY USE TEA IN COOKING?

Tea is finally breaking out of its familiar role as an accompaniment to afternoon tea fare and emerging as a provocative ingredient in every category on the menus of fine restaurants everywhere. More and more esteemed chefs around the country are bringing tea into the kitchen to create recipes using tea for entrées, desserts, or as a base for sophisticated new drinks, showing how infectious this "new" ingredient has become. Tea is an incredible flavor enhancer; it can be just the right addition to so many dishes from picnic favorites like chicken sandwiches or classic desserts like lemon tarts to traditional entrées using fish, meat, or even tofu with tea as a twist to delight any palate. Your senses will be engaged with the accent of a sweet Cameroon black, the intoxicating fragrance and taste of a classic Formosa oolong, the brisk biting edge of Ceylons like an Uva or Dimbula, or the mouth-cleansing finish of a Kenya.

With compelling evidence that both green and black teas have antioxidant properties, there is now a greater impetus to enjoy teas in the cup, and on the plate. This is a health-giving ingredient with a long history and an even brighter future—right in the home kitchen.

THE ORIGINS OF COOKING WITH TEA

Drinking tea was once enjoyed by a select few. Monks first introduced this beverage to their fellow practitioners. Then tea drinking spread to the royalty and finally to the public at large. Soon each country was experimenting with processing, adding flavorings, and eventually trying some innovative, albeit limited, ideas of cooking with tea. Japan gave us green tea ice cream, and thrifty housewives in Japan use leftover green tea in rice and broth or use fresh leaves as a garnish. The Burmese pickled the leaves for a biting salad called laphet, which is still common in some areas of Burma. The Chinese flavored the beverage with exquisite tiny rosebuds, adding a silky smoothness to black teas, and used fruits like lychee or flowers like chrysanthemum, orange blossoms (kweifruit), and osmanthus with refreshing results.

No food apparently escapes a little tea for flavoring. Some recipes China travelers have revealed to us include kidney beans with shrimp and a good dash of a fragrant pouchong such as Pi Lo Chun—a cross between a green and an oolong. Whole fish is a common dish in many of the Chinese cuisines. One idea is to stuff a cleaned whole fish with oolong tea and steam it with additional leaves and white wine. Another recipe uses one of the eight grades of China's most famous green tea, Dragonwell, to stir-fry with shredded chicken breast and bean sprouts. Perhaps the two most famous dishes created in mainland China are tea-marbled eggs and tea-smoked duck. The eggs get their marbling effect from being boiled in tea-infused water, which steeps into egg shells that have been lightly cracked on the second boil. Tea-smoked duck has as many recipes as there are Chinese chefs, and no respectable Chinese market or restaurant would be complete without this signature dish, as delicious as an entrée as it is in a salad.

HOW GREEN TEA BECAME BLACK

Although tea has been used in cooking in China for centuries, it is even more widely used as a beverage. What most Western countries know as tea is black tea, which was not then nor is it now what the Chinese drink. When tea was first introduced to Great Britain in the seventeenth century, the green tea that was shipped from China took months to arrive at Southampton. Green tea is more vulnerable than most teas to dampness, heat, and light, so what arrived was nearly unpalatable. Undaunted, the British didn't even consider drinking the tea, instead they cooked the leaves with eggs, salt, and butter and ate them. Not haute cuisine, but popular and allegedly satisfying.

China, reluctant to lose customers for its tea, created what we now know as black tea, tea that is completely dried and 100 percent oxidized of its vulnerable delicate green essence and water. The result is a richer-tasting tea able to last longer than its green brothers, especially on a ship from Canton to London. Thus, the staple tea most of us associate with Great Britain is not the "original" tea at all but a nod to marketing and the goal of a longer shelf life. As for the Chinese, they still drink green tea just as they did centuries ago and reserve the black tea for exporting throughout the world. They call "black" tea "red" to reflect the reddish hues of "black" or fully oxidized teas in the cup.

Whether your experience with tea is simply drinking a cup every once in a while or as an avid devotee, we invite you to share in our sense of discovery, to experience the fascination and excitement of cooking with tea. This "old" beverage easily translates as a "new" ingredient that adds an indefinable something to a dish, helps a recipe evolve into one that is beautifully compounded with flavor, or serves as a striking alternative to traditional herbs or spices. It is the goal of *Cooking with Tea* to demonstrate to both the seasoned and the amateur chef how healthful, interesting, and flavorful dishes made with teas can be. Our recipes are refreshing, innovative, and easy for anyone to prepare. And, best of all, tea is the ideal condiment: no calories, no sodium, no sugar, no fat—just pure flavor.

A Primer on Tea

What Is Tea?

All true tea comes from the same botanical plant, *Camellia sinensis*, and its varietals. The phenomena of style and type come from how the teas are dried and shaped—known as processing. What tea is not is a drink made from plants, trees, flowers, or other vegetation; these are herbal infusions, which, alas, are sometimes misleadingly referred to as herbal teas, but teas they are not.

True tea can be yellow, white, or green; it can be an oolong or a black or an aged tea called Pu-erh. Any of these teas can be scented or flavored with herbs, spices, fruits, or essential oils of flowers or fruits.

Theoretically, any tea can be blended with another. For example, greens can be blended with blacks, or several types of blacks can be blended together. The objective of blending is to capture all the flavor characteristics in one cup: flavor, aroma, and body. Not all teas boast all of these characteristics. Some teas are predominantly aromatic; others have expressive body or flavor. Some teas have much more of one characteristic than the other, hence blended teas are some of the most popular in the world, especially in packaged or tea bag form, which use lower-quality leaves and often need a little punch.

One of the most commonly known blends, English Breakfast, usually is a combination of black-processed China Keemun with Ceylon and Indian Assam, but blenders frequently use a combination of Kenya blacks with Darjeeling and Keemuns or other varieties. You can imagine the infinite possibilities that have helped to make teas such an exciting drink, blended or otherwise, for thousands of years.

China is the birthplace of tea, and many of its teas, from the green Dragonwells to black Yunnans, have become the touchstone against which other tea-growing countries are measured. Taiwan has created a process for tea, oolong, that is now world renowned. Few have mastered their techniques, although many have tried. Sri Lanka has its crisp, flavorful Ceylons, both as green or black; Japan has sweet greens, all made with exquisite care even when machinery is used; and India has countless delights from organic

Darjeelings or fine dark Assams to cloudless, fruit-filled iced teas made from pure Nilgiris, the essence of refreshment. What follows is a basic description of the most typical teas, many of which we use in our recipes.

TEA TYPES

Yellow and White Teas

Yellow, white, and green teas are not oxidized at all but are lightly air or steam dried. Whites and yellows use only the tiny leaf bud. Whites are primarily made in mainland China, although some limited whites or silvertips are being made from Assam and Darjeeling teas to great effect.

Green Teas

Mainland China makes what are perhaps the world's finest greens—delicate, sweet, grassy, and palate cleansing—running the gamut from their famous Lung Ching (Dragonwell) to the fragrant, more intense tasting green Yunnan with hundreds, maybe thousands, of greens in between.

Japanese green teas are lovely and exquisitely made. Green teas use the tenderest, youngest leaves and are steam dried and lightly shaped to retain not only their color but their intense spring-fresh flavor. The range is subtle but broad. From the delicate, sweet Gyokuro to the everyday refreshment of Sencha, Japanese greens are available in countless variations. Ones to seek out are the delicate Fukuyu, the light-tasting roasted teas like Hojicha and Bancha, or the delightful Genmaicha, made with rice and popcorn. All go so gently with Japanese foods and are nice counterpoints to spicy meals of other cuisines.

Black Teas

All tea was green tea before tea marketers realized that by drying the teas they could preserve them and lengthen their shelf life. So, ironically, now that green tea has regained its popularity, the largest producers of black teas, India and Sri Lanka, are now producing green teas. India's "new" greens

retain the wonderful bite that characterizes its teas, and one can find them in Assam, Darjeeling, and now Nilgiri in limited quantities. All of these "new" greens are processed in the style of Chinese greens without any oxidation whatsoever. Sri Lanka's Ceylon greens are clean tasting, have a nice full-mouth feel, and go wonderfully with all foods

Black teas are 100 percent oxidized and are the world's most commonly drunk teas as single estates, blends, or flavored teas. Their intensity makes them good foils for sugar and milk. However, the better made blacks are smooth, rich, and highly aromatic plain. Blacks are available in full leaf, broken leaf, and crushed or ground in the manufacturing process, called *CTC* (crush, tear, cut).

From the naturally fruity Cameroon to the never-clouding Indian Nilgiri, black teas are wonderful for iced drinks and hot cups of brew. Tea grows in more than thirty-five countries these days, so one can enjoy blacks like a crisp Kenyan, a rich, hearty Indonesian, a winey Keemun, or fragrant Yunnan (also available in green) from China and begin a fascinating journey around the world tasting teas.

Oolong Teas

Oolongs are oxidized from 2 to 80 percent, thus retaining an incredible fragrance and aromatic taste in the cup. Their leaves are usually quite large and flavorful and can be reinfused several times. Taiwan is a premier processor of oolongs, which are known by the former country name of Formosa. The Fujian Province of mainland China produces some exquisite oolongs, for example Ti Kwan Yin, and oolongs are being made from exceptional India teas, particularly Darjeelings from Makaibari Tea Estates and other prestigious farms in that country.

Showplace Teas

All of these teas are great to drink and to cook with, but one category in particular, the mudan, is a most charming tea to drink with any meal. These display teas make an elegant alternative to a cocktail, dessert wine, or after-dinner liqueur. They combine drama and great taste. Mudans are created in countless shapes but are generally served in the form of flowers that "blossom" when infused with water. Leaves are tied together, either with other leaves or light silk thread, and are shaped like a chrysanthemum, peonies, anemones, strawberries, a tiny bird's nest, or other delightful forms.

The other wonderful feature is that these mudans can be infused for a very long time, 20 to 30 minutes, in water considerably cooler than that used for hot tea beverages. A goblet of dried mudan in water can thus be placed in front of your guests during the entrée, and they can witness the "blossoming" during their meal. Mudans are generally green but also come in black teas, sometimes referred to as reds when Chinese teas are used.

Pu-erhs *("poo-err")*

Unique to China, this tea has often been dubbed the Chinese penicillin for its curative properties. What we do know is that it is a cholesterol cutter, a digestive aid, and a rich, dark, satisfying tea that is the perfect tea to wean coffee drinkers away from that black brew to the golden liqueur of tea leaves. It is intentionally aged, sometimes as long as 50 years, and a friendly bacteria is added. It is available in countless shapes, styles, and price ranges.

TIPS FOR BUYING AND STORING TEA

Because freshness is such an important criterion in purchasing tea, it's always a good idea to buy teas from a reputable store or mail-order source that turns over inventory quickly. Buy in small quantities, 2 to 4 ounces/60 to 115 grams, and use it quickly, at least within 3 months or less. The other benefit for buying small is that you can try a variety of different teas, and if one just isn't your cup, it's not such a tremendous loss.

Always think of tea as a food: buy fresh, store properly, and use quickly. Proper storage should be stainless steel or porcelain canisters with tight-fitting lids, stored in cool, dark, and dry cupboards, away from the enemies of tea: light, heat, moisture.

Brewing Tea

Water for Tea

Tea is all about water and leaf. From the moment the just-picked leaves begin their withering process, the objective is to remove moisture from the leaf, to make it ready to be shaped as a green leaf or to prepare it as an oolong or black tea with further heating and drying. The final step is for you, the consumer, to add water back to this fine leaf and have a nectar of a drink. Water, then, becomes as critical an ingredient in a cup of tea as the fine quality of the leaf itself. The ancient Chinese tea authority, Lu Yu, suggested waters from the ten famous springs of his country, but, alas, they are not available to us today. Instead, we have many choices of fine bottled spring waters, most of which make excellent tea.

If your city has fine tap water, please use that. Some communities, especially in the United States, have exceptional waters that are quite good for tea. In fact, a number of these cities bottle their waters for distribution elsewhere in the country.

The third choice would be to use tap water with a commercial filtering system attached to the water source.

Distilled water is ideal for irons, hair rollers, or clothing steamers precisely because it has no minerals or particles. What it does, when brewed for tea, is make a very flat, static taste.

One theory is that minerals are required to make the tea interact with the liquid; another theory is that the purer the water the more the true qualities of the tea will be revealed.

Still others have scientifically complicated reasons why one water is better than another. Personally, we believe that your own palate is the supreme judge. As with tea, water is also a matter of taste. Sample a variety of spring waters or tap waters and ask yourself what tastes best to you. Experiment, taste, try various temperatures and brewing times, and you will know.

Caffeine in Tea

Caffeine in teas is assimilated differently and over a slower period of time than caffeine in coffee. This difference is the reason why teas can both calm and provide alertness, while coffee only stimulates and energizes. Generally though, tea contains more caffeine than coffee. The big difference, however, is that a pound/kilogram of tea yields upwards of five times more cups than a pound/kilogram of coffee, making the per-cup amount of caffeine in tea one-fourth to one-fifth that of coffee.

A second factor is how teas are processed. White teas barely have any caffeine in them while greens, oolongs, and blacks have more.

A third barometer for caffeine is how the tea is infused. When brewing lightly with less-than-boiling water and for short periods of time (under 3 minutes), the tea yields considerably less cafeine than when boiling water is used for a period of 4 to 7 minutes to brew the tea leaves. If caffeine is a health concern, brew the tea and discard the liquor. Nearly 97 percent of the caffeine will be eliminated. Brew the leaves with a second infusion and drink that. Generally, cooking does not dissipate caffeine, so if you remain concerned, use only the second infusion when cooking with tea or drinking it.

Only a limited amount of research has been done on caffeine and theine in tea, and even less on how these naturally-occurring elements affect cooking. Theine, we do know, is an alkaloid, and alkaloids are stable elements that do not readily cook away as the alcohol content in a wine does.

What we have discovered is that

1   the alcohol content of a wine or sherry is considerably higher than the theine or caffeine content of the same amount of infused tea;

2   the amount of both theine and caffeine is relatively minor in the amounts of teas used in these recipes, and concern for caffeine and theine ingestion will be minuscule;

3   cooking methods determine the intensity of tea taste and theine and caffeine residue, but here again, the differences are so slight as to not be much of an issue.

- Gentle poaching using a tea-infused liquid retains more tea flavor and more theine.
- A tea-infused sauce would retain a little less theine, although as these sauces are reduced in volume, the theine concentration would increase slightly.
- An aromatic spice rub with tea retains slightly less theine in the dish than a simple tea-infused marinade because the tea does not penetrate beyond the surface of the food when the rub method is used.

It is our conclusion that there should be no concern about theine or caffeine when using tea in cooking. If you or a family member are exquisitely sensitive or supremely allergic to caffeine, infusing the tea twice and using only the liquid from the second infusion will eliminate 97% of the caffeine. Depending upon the cooking method you will have 3% or less of the caffeine, divided among the four or more portions of the recipe.

EQUIPAGE

Cooking with tea requires nothing unique in the way of equipment. However, we've found that the following items make everything easier and simpler. If you don't already own these classic tools, they are well worth the investment.

Chinois (fine-meshed sieve) This is excellent for straining solids, spices, and tea leaves from all mixtures. Because tea leaves are used only for flavoring and are not actually in our recipes, it's critical to have a fine-meshed sieve or strainer for this frequently requested technique.

Food processor or blender These are great time-saving appliances, particularly when making sauces or blending marinades, or for chopping and slicing large quantities of foods easily and uniformly.

French press-style tea infuser This handy device makes infusing teas a breeze and cleanup effortless. Place tea leaves in the infuser basket, pour on water, infuse, press water through the leaves, and pure, lovely, flavorful tea is the result every time. New glass teapots with swivel tea ball infusers are becoming more available.

Ice cream maker Canister or crank type, electric or battery-operated, the styles and types of ice cream makers provide the at-home chef with an easy, simple way to make the loveliest sorbets, granitas, and ice creams. At fine department stores and cook shops everywhere.

Measuring tools Measuring cups for liquid and dry ingredients and measuring spoons are essential for baking and important for cooking. All ingredients should be leveled unless otherwise indicated.

Mortar and pestle or spice grinder The electric or battery-operated grinders certainly save time and elbow grease, but the classic mortar and pestle somehow infuses your spirit into the spices. Whenever possible, buy spices whole and in small quantities and process as desired. Nothing tastes better than freshly ground spices!

Recycling tub This is a clever way to discard your spent tea leaves. Set aside a ceramic or plastic tub for all your used tea leaves. Tea is ultimately recyclable, so you can toss them onto the compost, sprinkle around indoor or outdoor plants, or dry them and scatter on Fido's or Kitty's bed to ward off fleas.

Springform cake and tart pans These make presentation easier. Traditional tart and cake pans are fine; just line them with parchment paper and use aerosolized oil to coat.

Stainless steel bowls These are simply the best. They are easy to find, inexpensive, and can be used so many ways. We always use them over a pot of boiling water in lieu of a double boiler. This affords more room to whisk together ingredients and avoids double boiler burns or uneven cooking spots.

Timer Although most teas are forgiving, it is important to infuse by the clock, not by color or aroma. Find a timer that has at least 30 minutes on it.

Whisk For stirring, mixing, or blending in bowls or saucepans, nothing works better or more efficiently than stainless steel wire whisks. They're available in many sizes and from stiffly wired to flexible balloon shapes.

Wok Available at fine cookware shops everywhere and in both Chinese and Japanese food markets, woks are great for smoking with tea. It is critical to get a tight-fitting lid and to use a rack with a screen to prevent small items of food from falling through. We suggest a splatter shield, pizza rack, or screened rack for use over smoking ingredients used in a wok. The wire grid of a traditional rack is too widely spaced and using it may result in much food falling down into the smoking ingredients.

Wooden spoons These are very good for stirring cream-based sauces and to test for doneness (a sauce is done when it coats the bowl or back of the spoon). Get several in different sizes; they're indispensable. They're also the best tool for pressing down tea leaves to make sure every precious drop of the infusion goes into your recipe.

How to Brew Tea for Drinking

The recipe for a good cup of tea to drink varies with the type of tea you are using. If you only use tea bags, 1 tea bag per person with 6 ounces/180ml of boiling water should provide a good cup. If using green tea, use water almost to boiling.

For loose-leaf teas, the amount of tea used should be weighed rather than measured. Some tea leaves are small and heavy while others are huge yet very light, requiring many leaves to provide good flavor in the cup.

To prepare for your cup of tea, rinse out the cup with very hot water and set it aside. Rinse out a teapot with hot water and set it aside. Measure out the tea, test the water for the right temperature, and pour over the tea leaves in the pot. Brew for 1 minute; taste. Brew longer to suit your taste. All professional tea merchants will give you guidelines for the quantity of tea to use and the length of time to brew it. If he or she won't take the time to give you this information, seek another vendor.

We generally use 1 teaspoon of tea leaves for 6 ounces of water, adding nearly twice that much for white teas. Boiling water should only be used for Pu-erh or a very hearty black. All other teas should be brewed with nearly boiling water, from 175 to 200°F/79 to 85°C. Boiling water leeches out too much flavor too quickly, often scalding the leaves and making the brew unnecessarily bitter. (See chart below.) You can boil the water, let it cool to the desired temperature, then prepare your tea with that water. If you prefer, you can heat the water only to the desired temperature. Experimenting with your tea kettle and a food thermometer will give you an idea of when the temperature is just right if you don't have an electric tea kettle that gives a digital reading of water temperatures.

Temperature and steeping times are also critical to a great cup of tea. The following are *only* guidelines; always ask your tea merchant about suggested times and temperatures if you are unfamiliar with the tea. Both whites and greens can be steeped longer on subsequent steepings. High quality whites and greens will offer at least three steepings, often more. Please experiment to find what you like best.

whites should barely be steeped, about 30 seconds in 175 to 185°F/79 to 85°C water.
greens should be steeped 30 to 45 seconds in 185 to 190°F/85 to 88°C water.
oolongs should be steeped 1 to 3 minutes in 190°F/88°C water.
blacks can be steeped 2 to 5 minutes in 195 to 200°F/91 to 93°C water.
pu-erhs should be steeped 3 to 5 minutes in rolling boiling water (212°F/96°C).

If you follow these directions, when you take a sip of your tea you will know immediately what true tea taste really is.

So, how does one brew a cup of tea for drinking? First, buy the best tea you can afford, take enough time to brew it properly, and savor it slowly. Tea, and you, are worth this modest effort for enormous pleasure.

HOW TO BREW TEA FOR COOKING

The most critical challenge in cooking with tea is how to get the most flavor from the tea without unleashing the harsh astringency so common when tea leaves are left too long in water. Certainly, if a tea is undrinkable, it should not be used in cooking.

There are certain techniques for cooking with tea. Most important is not to use leftover tea and not to brew tea to extra strength.

For most of our recipes, we brew tea lightly in 185°F/85°C water for 1 to 3 minutes. This is a quick and easy technique, especially if you do not have loads of leisure time to cook. If you have a filtered hot water faucet on your sink, you can even have it adjusted to a constant 185°F/85°C.

In other recipes, the tea is infused and then reheated or cooked with other ingredients without sacrificing quality, because it was gently brewed the first time. This two-step process is possible by using teas chosen for their ability to be steeped longer without becoming bitter.

In some recipes, particularly ones using a protein, we infuse tea in boiling water, cream, or juice for a brief time to extract the fullest flavor of the tea into foods. If you can cook leisurely, then please consider the more traditional way of cooking with tea: Use cold water to infuse the leaves, even for up to 2 hours, which results in the best, most flavorful extraction with absolutely no bitterness no matter what type of tea is brewed. Using 2 tea-spoons/10 grams of leaves for every 8 ounces/240 milliliters of cold water enables you to extract more tea flavor.

Yes, there are exceptions, depending on the type of tea used and the recipe. Sometimes infusing the tea leaves for either a shorter or longer time may work better. Cold extraction teas can be quickly reduced over high heat to concentrate their flavor just before adding them at the last minute to a dish or to a stock or braising liquid, thereby maximizing the burst of flavor it gives to your special dish.

When tea is used as a tenderizer (marinades for meats and poultry, for example) the proportion of leaves to liquid may be even higher than 2 teaspoons/10 grams to 8 ounces/240 milliliters of water. When tea is used as a marinade for a long period of time, it generates a greater intensity of flavor. For all these ways of infusing foods with teas, please refer to the Essential Techniques chapter, or read our recipes using such techniques prior to your individual explorations.

You'll recognize many correlations between cooking with wine and cooking with tea. The "long finish" wine connoisseurs speak of is true for tea and will have your guests asking "What's the wonderful flavoring in this dish?"

TEAS USED IN THIS BOOK

We have chosen teas for the recipes in this book based on both their flavor and their availability. As always, we encourage you to experiment with tastes you enjoy in these and other recipes you create.

Assam (Tippy Assam) Assam is the strong soldier of tea, though there have been some uniquely processed white Assams. It's hearty, fragrant, and stands up beautifully to milk and in recipes for hearty foods. An ideal tea for blending with those teas that need a little punch, Assam brews to golden or red gold liquor. The Tippy Assam used in some of our recipes has a particularly malty, almost chocolaty essence.

Cameroon This lesser-known tea from West Africa is a real find: rich, smooth, sweet, able to stand up well to other ingredients in cooking. It is also a marvelous afternoon tea on its own with nothing added to it. Very mellow and fruity, this is a deep, rich, and vanilla-like tea that blends beautifully with both sweet and savory dishes.

Ceylon From Sri Lanka, Ceylon teas are available in both green and black, each with that crisp, brisk, clean taste that marks these island teas. They are lighter than their Indian cousins and brighter than their distant Chinese relatives. A reliable classic for the tea cupboard or to use in a variety of dishes you cook with tea.

Darjeeling Home to about 86 tea estates, this region in the state of West Bengal in northeast India lies at the foothills of the fabled Himalayas.

The blessings of geography provide these teas with a distinctive delicate/ sharp fragrance matched with a taste that is, when properly brewed, simply divine. Often referred to as the champagne of teas, it requires a minimal time for brewing and the liquors range from golden yellow to golden red. Various processes are used, from green to oolong to black. The resulting tastes offer many choices for drinking these teas alone or for cooking with them in a way that adds both fragrance and taste. Elegant and suave are two adjectives that cry out to be applied to this tea.

Muscatel Darjeeling is named for the muscat grape it sometimes favors. It is tea plucked between the first and second flush (or plucking) of the season. After the first flush, the bushes relax and become dry and brown. Then the fast-moving norwesters sweep up from the Bay of Bengal to unleash intense cloudbursts for very short periods of time, and, overnight, Darjeeling turns a riot of green. Usually 20 percent of the freshly emerging second flush shoots are stymied but not killed by this change in weather, but all is not lost. These stunted leaves can be carefully segregated and manufactured in a special way. The result is a muscatel Darjeeling—available only for three to four weeks in May and June. A particularly good example of muscatel Darjeeling comes from the Makaibari Tea Estates.

Earl Grey Imperial Who hasn't enjoyed the elegance of bergamot-flavored black tea blends? The Imperial is several steps up the taste bud ladder and offers a very sophisticated taste without the unpleasant tang of commercial artificial flavorings. Bergamot is a pear-shaped citrus fruit found in the Mediterranean, and in a tea it should accent but not overpower the combination of teas, usually Keemun, Assam, Ceylon, or other combinations of traditional black teas.

English Breakfast Blend Perhaps the most popular blend in the world, it is readily available in tea bags, but seek out those tins or bulk sources of loose-leaf blends for excellent flavor. Generally, this blend has Keemun for color and rich aroma, Ceylon for briskness and bite, and Assam for intensity of taste. Lately, Kenya and other fine blacks have found their way into this blend. You can make your own, too, by mixing three of these black teas to your taste. Start with equal portions of each and adjust as you would seasonings.

Genmaicha This green tea from Japan is fun, light, and goes with a variety of meals. The fun comes from the visual sight and the taste of popcorn and rice intertwined with fresh green tea. It's available everywhere and usually quite moderately priced. Roasted, nutty, and grassy, this tea sings of spring.

Jasmine Although some black teas are scented with these intoxicating flowers, the finest Chinese jasmine teas are made with green or pouchong tea leaves, providing a delicate, faintly aromatic experience that is incredible. The liquor generally brews up quite pale, almost with no color at all, and the fragrance lingers for quite a while. Jasmine Yin Hao is a superior grade with an exquisite fragrance and taste. Jasmine Pearls is another style to seek out. This tea's well-rounded sweetness and refreshing perfume adds a layer of complexity to everything from rich fish steaks to creamy chocolate mousse. Do *not* use teas made with Jasmine oils or artificial flavorings, used by many blenders. They may heighten the aroma, but they alter the taste considerably and are not recommended for cooking.

Kanyam Golden Nepal Many teas grown north of India, in Sikkim and Nepal, reflect the intrinsic Darjeeling character of their nearby cousins. Kanyam Golden Nepal is no exception. Its aroma adds an elegance to its luxurious, lightly astringent taste so typical of the finest Darjeelings. Drink this one absolutely plain to absorb all the flavor notes.

Keemun When this China black is good it's magnificent, and when it's bad it's pretty darn good. Look for tea leaves that smell intense, almost sweet, and are consistently sized. It brews up a glorious deep red, which is why the Chinese call fully oxidized teas red teas (what Westerners refer to as black). Keemun makes a good tea for cooking because its soft edge of flavor blends in so well with spices and adds a definitive sweetness to most dishes.

Kenya This black tea continues to surprise because of its reliable taste, constant and plentiful supply, and good price. Kenyans grow fabulous coffee (mainly for export), too, but it's interesting to note that what Kenyans drink is tea! If looking for a classic, clean-tasting black tea for drinking or cooking, this one is perfect.

Lapsang Souchong Hundreds of varieties of this tea are made throughout the world, but the original began in mainland China as an error; some black tea was dried too close to a bonfire and was considered unsellable. Fortunately, someone decided to brew some up and serve it, and, voilà, a tradition was born. Some are quite intense; others are made not over wood but rubber and who knows what, so opt for reliable blenders or the best your tea merchant has to offer. Some brands to try are Hu-Kwa from Mark T. Wendell, Fortnum & Mason, and bulk from various on-line tea merchants. Its obvious smokiness is an asset when one wishes to add a sweet, charred edge to foods.

Lung Ching (Dragonwell) Many tea lovers consider Lung Ching to be the premier green tea of mainland China; it is sweet, fresh, delicate, and mouth pleasing. It is available in many grades, but even the lowly ones are refreshing to the palate.

Lychee This is a classic scented Chinese tea using the sweet essence of the round, flesh-colored fruit common to both China and India. We use few scented or flavored teas in our recipes but this one is wonderful.

Masala Chai This tea drink of India is brewed in milk with a mix of spices ranging from pepper to cardamom to cinnamon. The proper name is masala chai, because chai literally means tea, so to say chai tea is redundant. Masala is also referred to as a spice mixture in Indian cooking. Often, a lower quality, 100-percent dried black tea is used in the making of masala chai, which is cooked for a long time. Masala chai is usually served from backpack samovars by street tea vendors called chaiwallas, who seem to be at every train stop or bazaar in India, offering a bit of nourishment for pennies. This peppery tea blend is also good with a base of fine Indian Nilgiri. Chai is available in concentrates, powders, ready-to-drink, and loose-leaf with spices to which you add sweetener, water, and milk to taste. A lingering, spicy sweetness is its strength as an ingredient in cooking. The concentrates are convenient for baking because you can use just a tablespoon/15 milliliters or more to give dough a wonderful kick without the necessity of cooking up a big batch of masala chai.

Nilgiri A wonderful clean-tasting tea from India, Nilgiri is exceptional for its brisk taste as a stand-alone tea, offering the chef so many possibilities for use in baking and cooking. Previously relegated to blending status, this Merlot of tea offers a nice balance when served with the traditional English afternoon tea service. Nilgiri teas brew a liquor that is a golden color with a sweet fragrance.

Oolong Wuyi Suixin is a supremely fine oolong, highly aromatic and flavorful and worth every penny. Another fine oolong to seek is Ti Kwan Yin. Oolongs should be young and fresh because their full-mouth feel and distinct aromas fade quickly. The best are from Taiwan (Formosa).

Sencha Generally referred to as the everyday green tea of Japan, Sencha comes in a wide spectrum of grades, some flavored with flowers or fruits, and each a provocative taste and quite pretty to view. Most Senchas are pleasantly grassy, should be brewed very lightly, and drunk plain. In cooking, it adds a freshness and a light astringency that freshens the palate as it pleases all the senses.

Thai Tea This is the classic tea served in Thai restaurants. A black tea, it is usually flavored with vanilla, star anise, and corn, with condensed milk added for iced versions. Alternative selections would be vanilla, or any finely powdered black tea scented with vanilla or star anise. Two selections from Mariage Frères or Chado would fit the bill: St. Marc or Eros, seductively scented and exquisite, or make your own vanilla tea as suggested below.

Vanilla This tea is usually found with a strong black from commercial tea blenders, or you can make your own by adding a whole vanilla bean pod to a container of strong, dry black tea leaves and let stand overnight or longer. Other teas with the sweet essence of vanilla are Mauritius and Cameroon, for times when you want to use a sweet but not sugary tea to infuse a dish. *Yunnan* Available both as a green or a black, Yunnan has a natural sweet edge that makes it ideal for breakfast tea or as a blender with more brisk teas. It's very effective in both entrées and desserts to soften spices or other ingredients in the dish. Dark and deep with a lasting aroma and flavor, this tea adds a memorable touch to poultry dishes and stands up well in vegetable sides with members of the brassica family (broccoli, broccoflower, cabbages, Asian greens).

Cooking with Tea: Essential Techniques

How to Choose Tea as an Ingredient for a Recipe

First and foremost, use your nose. If the tea is aromatic, fills your nose with the heady scent of a bosky forest or a green glade, then it's apt to stand up to being combined with other seasonings and ingredients in a dish. If it's utterly scent-free, then it's beyond its prime; it's stale and has probably been exposed to harsh light or heat, or perhaps it began as a tea of poor quality and dull flavor. Toss out that tea and find something better.

Our caveat: If it doesn't look fresh and doesn't smell fresh, it isn't fresh. Tea used in cooking should be considered as important as any produce.

Freshness, good color, lively to the touch, all those qualities important to selecting fresh greens, vegetables, and fruits are critical to look for in tea suitable for both drinking and cooking. Use teas during their season at their peak flavor, just as you would choose fruits and vegetables in their seasons. This is no place to cheat your palate; use the finest teas you can afford and brew them carefully.

Loose-leaf gourmet teas are suggested for each recipe simply because the best ingredients make the best dish. The amounts used in each recipe are modest in both quantity and price so that anyone can afford the luxury of gourmet teas. We urge you to experiment; try teas you've never tasted before; enjoy their far-reaching flavor potential as both a beverage and an ingredient in foods.

The teas used in these recipes are truly affordable luxuries. For pennies you can add even the most expensive tea to a recipe. Fine tea shops, mail-order catalogs, and on-line sources are sprouting up throughout the country to make gourmet teas truly accessible no matter where you live. One phone call, fax, or e-mail can bring the finest teas in the world right to the door of any kitchen as early as tomorrow morning. (See Appendix E: Resources for Connoisseur Teas and Teapots for details.)

How to Use Tea in Cooking

Our experiments have led us to the conclusion that the brewed tea liquor is an exquisite ingredient to infuse creams, juices, gravies, and other liquids for sauces and marinades. Tea's innate flavor is easily transferred and is economical, easily available, and simple to use.

Fats, in general, are the flavor carriers, so cream is an ideal element for a tea-infused sauce served with desserts. One only needs a tablespoon/14 grams of leaves or so to give drama and dazzle to a dish, so do splurge a little when making desserts.

The acidity of apple juice, lemon, orange, or other citrus juices also works well in bringing out the flavor characteristics of most teas. Producing an infusion first then adding it to the final dish, sans the leaves, is easy, neat, and adds the punch of flavor without calories. After a few experiments creating tea-infused sauces you will readily understand how tea is a perfect condiment for enhancing the flavor of any dish, savory or sweet. It contributes an elegance that is often mysterious in fragrance and taste, yet it is just plain easy to do.

In the end, however, it is the essence of the tea that is transferred to your dish, and this is done by: braising, infusing, rubs, and smoking, among other ways. We use these particular techniques many times in our recipes, and we encourage you to embrace these easy ways to cook with tea.

Braising

In classical cooking, braising is a moist cooking method in which the foods being cooked are barely submerged and the liquid never exceeds a simmer. In this case, it's a gentle, light way of infusing foods with the essence of tea. Braising helps to tenderize, flavor, and enhance the taste of the poultry, beef, or vegetables being infused.

*4 tablespoons/2 ounces black tea
    leaves of your choice*

2 quarts/2 liters spring water

*Fruity olive oil, enough to coat the
    pan for searing*

*4 cloves garlic, smashed then
    finely chopped*

*1 1/2 cups/250 grams thinly sliced yel-
    low onions (one large onion)*

*1/2 cup/100 grams packed
    brown sugar*

*1/2 cup/120 milliliters stewed
    tomatoes or fresh chopped
    tomatoes*

2 1/2 pounds/1 kilogram of chicken

*Salt and freshly ground pepper
    to taste*

Braising Recipe

Preheat the oven to 325°F (163°C). Prepare the tea by brewing it in cool (170°F/77°C) water, then sieve out the leaves and set aside. Sauté the garlic and onions in the olive oil until softened. Add the sugar and tomatoes and stir until sugar dissolves. To braise, place the chicken in a large pan or Dutch oven, season with salt and pepper to taste, then cover with the sautéed mixture. Add the brewed tea, then bake, covered, until chicken is tender, about 1 to 1½ hours and tests done by thermometer—164°F (73°C). This braising liquid can also be used for other meats, poultry, or vegetables, but cooking times differ greatly according to the cuts of meat or the quantity and type of vegetables. Adjust accordingly.

Infusing

Citrus juices such as lemon, orange, or grapefruit take well to assertive black tea infusions with Keemun, Assam, or Cameroon in particular, and apple juice is wonderful, especially as a sauce with poultry or pork. Cream, because of its fat content, absorbs the infusion of teas beautifully, and its delicate taste works with greens, oolongs, or blacks with equal aplomb.

Juice Infusion

1 cup/250 milliliters juice

1 tablespoon/14 grams tea, such as Kenya, Ceylon black, or China black (for more intense tea flavor, opt for Assam, Cameroon, or Keemun)

In a small saucepan, heat the juice until boiling then remove from the heat. Add the tea leaves and infuse for up to 10 minutes. Sieve out the leaves and add seasonings as desired for an entrée. For a dessert sauce, add sugar to taste then thicken with about a teaspoon of cornstarch dissolved in 1 tablespoon of cold water, simmering lightly until cornstarch and sugar are dissolved. Mask over dessert or serve on the side.

Cream Infusion

4 ounces/120 milliliters heavy cream

1 tablespoon/14 grams black tea leaves, such as Assam

In a heavy 1-quart/1-liter saucepan, bring cream and tea leaves to a boil then remove from heat. Infuse for 1 hour at room temperature. Over a bowl, pass the mixture through a fine-meshed sieve, pressing hard on the tea leaves to extract as much of the tea-infused cream as possible. Sweeten if desired and use as a sauce for desserts by masking a plate with 1 tablespoon (5 milliliters) of the sauce and reserving some to garnish the dessert. We suggest Assam tea, but Keemun or any other assertive black will do. If you would like to use a green, consider the delicacy of a Chinese Dragonwell or the essence of Japanese Sencha. For pure perfume, consider the divine fragrance of a Formosa Jasmine Green against the thick sweet cream.

Rubs

Any combination of complementary spices can be used in a rub, which acts as a crust for firm-fleshed fish, meats, and poultry. The following rub is suitable for $1\frac{1}{2}$ pounds/750 grams of fish, meat, or poultry. Adjust seasonings to your taste; it's fun to experiment!

Basic Tea Rub

4 tablespoons/2 ounces black tea leaves (Kenya, Kanyam Nepal, Ceylon Uva are good choices)

$\frac{1}{2}$ teaspoon/1 gram ground ginger

1 cinnamon stick

$\frac{1}{2}$ teaspoon/1 gram whole coriander seeds

$\frac{1}{4}$ teaspoon/500 milligrams whole black peppercorns

1 tablespoon/14 grams brown sugar

$\frac{1}{2}$ teaspoon/3 grams salt

In an electric spice grinder or with a mortar and pestle, combine and process all of the ingredients until a fine powder results. Spread out on a plate and set aside. Lightly oil fish or meat then dip pieces in the rub and set aside for a minimum of 15 minutes to form the crust. Cook as desired, preferably pan searing or baking in the oven until done.

Smoking

A smoky-flavored tea, like Lapsang Souchong, can impart its smokiness to foods when used either as a marinade or added to the wood chips or charcoal after they have whitened, then cooled somewhat. However, smoking foods *with* tea is another technique. Here's how to do it:

Whether using a buffet-size batch of vegetables for stir-frying or blanching, or moist steaming a whole fish, a well-seasoned, roomy wok is the tool of choice for this bit of culinary magic.

For best results in a wok, do not crowd the pan with too much food. A good rule of thumb is no more than a pound of food at one time. This provides for freer circulation of the smoke inside the wok, resulting in more uniform flavor and color.

The fat or lean quality of food, plus the bone structure, influences how much, if any, additional cooking may be required following smoking. The ingredients used to create the smoke in the wok will usually incinerate before most foods are fully cooked, so you need to remove the incinerated mixture and replace it with a new supply. Continue to smoke or opt for finishing the dish in an oven, steamer, sauté pan, or grill, as desired. Always use the exhaust fan over your stove before, during, and after the smoking process. If the weather permits, open some windows so excess smoke can escape from the kitchen.

Foods at room temperature acquire the deepest smoky flavor, so allow at least 10 to 20 minutes for foods to warm up to room temperature if refrigerated.

Smoking Mixture

*This recipe will impart a light to medium smoky taste and is suitable for one
pound of boneless meat, poultry, fish, vegetables, or pasta.*

1 cup/240 milliliters raw white rice

1/4 cup/50 grams packed brown sugar

*1 cup/225 grams fragrant loose
    tea (Lapsang Souchong, Yunnan,
    or Jasmine)*

1 cinnamon stick

6 whole star anise pods

6 cloves

1 sweet apple, cut into eight wedges

*1 strip of orange peel, about 4
    inches/10 centimeters long*

*(Fragrant herbs like fresh rosemary,
    thyme, or oregano can be added to
    the blend as desired, or the sugar
    and aromatics can be increased to
    sweeten the smoky flavor.)*

Line the inside of the bottom of a wok with a crisscross of heavy-duty foil, including a 3-inch/7.5-centimeter overhang on all sides. Similarly line the inside of the lid.

Outfit the wok with a wire rack with legs that will lift it at least 1/2 inch/13 millimeters off the bottom of the wok.

Combine all the ingredients and spread evenly in a thin layer on the foil in the wok. Place the foods to be smoked on the rack. Cover the wok tightly, crimping the foil that extends from the base and the lid of the wok.

Heat the wok over high heat until the first wisps of smoke emerge from the wok. Place rack in wok then cover tightly and cook 5 minutes for a light smoking, 10 to 15 minutes for a medium smoking. Repeat as necessary.

To smoke foods longer than 15 minutes, replace the original batch of smoking ingredients with successive batches. Otherwise, the smoking ingredients will burn and adversely affect the dish.

One pound of bone-in chicken breasts, for example will require from 25 to 35 minutes of high heat in a fully smoking wok. Test by inserting a knife into the thickest part of the breast to make sure the juices are clear. An instant-read thermometer should show 165 to 170°F/ 74 to 77°C at the thickest point away from the bone.

Stocks

Fresh stock is easy and quick to make and keeps in the refrigerator for at least 3 days. If you prefer, it keeps well in the freezer for about a month.

Vegetable Stock

This all-purpose stock is great for boosting flavor without a lot of calories and works wonderfully with many of our tea sauces. The vegetables listed are suggestions only, but a nice balance of root vegetables, fresh greens, and seasonings represents the core of any good freshly made stock. The stock does not contain salt because we use it in the recipes themselves.

2 medium carrots, unpeeled, washed, then cut into thick chunks

2 stalks of celery

1 onion, roughly chopped

1 cup/225 grams loosely packed chard, spinach, or similar greens

1 pound/500 grams root vegetables (any assortment of large celery root, rutabaga, parsnip, or parsley root)

Olive oil for sweating

3 quarts/3 liters water

4 cloves

1 bay leaf

3 cloves garlic, lightly smashed

1/2 teaspoon/500 milligrams dried thyme

1 tablespoon/5 grams whole black peppercorns, smashed

Wash and clean the vegetables and chop roughly. In a heavy stockpot over low heat, sweat vegetables in olive oil until softened and light golden brown, about 10 minutes. Add the water and seasonings and cook over medium heat for about 1 hour. Sieve out the vegetables and store in the refrigerator in a clean container or covered bowl until needed. Final quantity will be reduced down to about 1 to $1\frac{1}{2}$ quarts/1 liter to 1.5 liters of intensely flavored stock.

Now that we've given you an overview of what tea is, how to drink it, and how to cook with it, it's time to apply the techniques and the tea to something wonderful for dinner tonight. Bon appétit!

part two

The Recipes

Starters, Condiments, Complements, and Asides

Darjeeling Peach Conserve

Foie Gras with Tea-Infused Apricots

Jade Shrimp in Lung Ching Tea

Jasmine-Cured Salmon with Lime-Mustard Sauce

Rata-tea-ouille

Red Rice in Oolong Tea

Smoked Chicken Salad with Tea Vinaigrette

Spring Rolls with Thai Tea Sauce

Tea-Cured Salmon and Ginger Sandwich

Tea-Poached Plums

Tea-Smoked Mushrooms

Tea-Wilted Greens with Summer Fruit and Goat Cheese

Darjeeling Peach Conserve

This jam is a lovely complement to the fruity character of fine Darjeeling tea. It's great served with scones, shortbread, or morning toast. Best of all, it can be made in advance and stored in the refrigerator for at least a month. During the season, use the freshest, ripest, and most fragrant peaches you can find. Out of season, canned peaches in fruit syrup (no extra sugar added) will do. Frozen peaches work well. This jam is not just for sweets; it makes a wonderful glaze for poultry or ham.

2 teaspoons/10 grams loose-leaf Darjeeling tea

16 ounces/500 milliliters water

4 pounds/1.8 kilograms fresh peaches, peeled, pitted, and roughly chopped. If using canned peaches, drain well; for frozen peaches, defrost thoroughly and drain well.

2 pounds/1 kilogram granulated white sugar

$1/_2$ cup/75 grams chopped crystallized ginger

Steep 2 teaspoons/10 grams of tea leaves for 3 minutes in 16 ounces/ 500 milliliters of water heated to 180°F/82°C. Drain off liquor from the leaves. You should have 2 cups/500 milliliters of brewed tea.

Place all the ingredients except the crystallized ginger into a heavy 3-quart/3-liter saucepan. Bring to a boil, skimming frequently during the first few minutes of cooking.

Reduce heat and cook just until the mixture coats the spoon then flows off slowly, about 15 minutes. Sauce should have the appearance of a very thin syrup.

Add the crystallized ginger. Cook for about 15 minutes, stirring fre- quently. This mixture will not appear thick when hot, but does set some when cool. It is not designed to be as firm as commercially made jams. Yields about $1^1/_2$ quarts.

Foie Gras with Tea-Infused Apricots

The fruity, tea-infused sauce is used twice, once to poach the apricots and once in combination with a tawny port to sauce the extravagant appetizer. The yin and yang of the bite of exotic spices against the silky smooth sauce sets up the palate for the next delectable taste of a quintessential luxury food—foie gras. Try this one when you want to celebrate, like the fact that today is a Monday...

*1 tablespoon/14 grams lychee
    tea leaves or other lightly scented
    tea like a vanilla, Mauritius,
    or Cameroon*

1 quart water

*4 whole apricots, use dried
    apricots when fresh apricots
    are out of season*

*1 pound (16 ounces/500 grams) duck
    foie gras*

1/2 teaspoon/3 grams salt

1/4 teaspoon/1 gram pepper

1/4 teaspoon/1 gram ground cloves

1/4 teaspoon/1 gram ground coriander

1/4 teaspoon/1 gram cinnamon

Pinch of chili pepper

1 cup/250 milliliters vegetable stock

1/4 cup/60 milliliters tawny port

*1 tablespoon/15 grams sweet
    (unsalted) butter*

*1 teaspoon/5 grams lychee tea
    for seasoning*

*Garnish: pinch of coarse salt and four
    slices of egg bread, toasted*

Brew the tea leaves in hot water (185°F/85°C) for about 2 minutes, then drain through a fine-meshed sieve, pressing hard on the tea leaves to extract as much of the infusion as possible. Place the tea in a heavy saucepan and slowly poach the apricots for 10 to 15 minutes over a very low simmering heat. (This technique works equally well for either fresh or dried apricots.)

Remove the apricots from the heat and set aside to cool. Reserve 1 cup/250 milliliters of the poaching liquid. When cool enough to handle, remove the peels, carefully cut apricots in half, and gently remove the pits.

Slice the foie gras into 8 diagonal slabs (cross cuts). Combine the salt, pepper, cloves, coriander, cinnamon, and chili pepper together and rub into the foie gras. Place the slices in a dry heavy skillet that has been heated almost to smoking. Sear the sliced foie gras over high heat, turning once after about 2 minutes until lightly browned. Remove foie gras from pan and gently lay on paper towels to drain.

Pour off the excess fat accumulated in the pan and deglaze with a combination of 1 cup/250 milliliters of the poaching tea liquid and 1 cup/250 milliliters of the vegetable broth. Add the port and continue to simmer until liquid is reduced to about 3/4 cup/180 milliliters. For added flavor, add 1 tablespoon/15 grams of butter, in small bits, whisking thoroughly until completely melted, then add in 1 teaspoon/5 grams of lychee tea leaves and sieve out the leaves as you present the appetizer as described below.

Assembly: Place two slices of foie gras on each plate and garnish with a pinch of coarse salt. Lay 2 halves of apricots against the slabs, then mask with the mixture of reduced port, vegetable broth, and tea. Add toast points made from an egg bread such as brioche or challah, sliced on the diagonal. Serves 4.

Jade Shrimp in Lung Ching Tea

With its grassy, almost herbal personality, brewed Chinese Lung Ching
(also known as Dragonwell) green tea creates a pleasing foil for briny shrimp.
This is a colorful and highly aromatic dish.

2 quarts/2 liters water

1 ounce/30 grams loose-leaf Lung
*   Ching tea*

1 pound/500 grams peeled and
*   deveined medium shrimp (leave*
*   tails on for presentation)*

1 tablespoon/15 milliliters sesame oil

1 large clove garlic, peeled and
*   smashed to release its aroma*

1 ounce/30 grams fresh ginger
*   root, peeled and thinly sliced*

2 pounds/1 kilogram fresh spinach
*   leaves, with stems removed and*
*   discarded, washed and dried*

Salt to taste

2 tablespoons/3 grams sesame seeds,
*   lightly toasted*

Garnishes: julienned yellow and red
*   peppers and finely slivered scallions*

Bring the water to just under a boil (about 185°F/85°C). Add the tea and the shrimp and cook over low heat at the barest simmer for about 3 to 4 minutes, or until the shrimp are opaque. Remove from heat and let stand until cool. While steeping in the tea-scented poaching liquid, the shrimp gains additional flavor. When cool, refrigerate.

Just before serving, heat the sesame oil in a heavy skillet and add the garlic and ginger root. Cook for about 20 seconds or just until the garlic and ginger root release their aroma. Do not burn.

Add the spinach and salt to taste and cook just until the spinach brightens in color and barely wilts. Drain and put spinach in a bowl or on a platter, arrange chilled shrimp on top, sprinkle with sesame seeds, and garnish with the yellow and red peppers. Sprinkle all with the scallions. Serves 4 appetizer-sized portions.

Jasmine-Cured Salmon with Lime-Mustard Sauce

This is a beautiful dish for entertaining that's colorful, delicious, and easy to prepare. Suitable for a party of 30, this recipe is also possible for a smaller piece of fish such as a 2-pound center cut of salmon. Halve the seasonings accordingly. Pairing it with an exquisite Jasmine Pearl served in white or celadon cups makes a perfect companion.

Jasmine Salmon

1 whole fresh salmon, filleted, with skin left on, head removed, 4 to 5 pounds/2 to 2.5 kilograms

Olive oil to lightly coat fish

4 ounces/115 grams Jasmine green tea, pulverized (save some whole leaf for a garnish)

2 cups/450 grams kosher salt

2 large onions, thinly sliced

1 tablespoon/12 grams black pepper, coarsely ground

$\frac{1}{2}$ cup/100 grams granulated sugar

4 bunches fresh dill, roughly chopped, stems removed

Garnishes: edible flowers such as nasturtiums or pansies; thinly sliced dark bread or pita toasts, or both; 6 lemon and 6 lime wedges

Lime-Mustard Sauce

Juice of 4 limes

4 teaspoons/20 milliliters Dijon mustard

Brown sugar to taste

Freshly ground black pepper to taste

Salt to taste

1 cup/250 milliliters fruity virgin olive oil

Remove as many of the remaining bones as possible from the fish using pliers or tweezers. Lightly rub the fish with olive oil, then rub with powdered tea leaves. Add sugar, onions, and dill. Coat with pepper and salt. Do this equally to both sides of the fish. Put 2 pieces back to back and cover with a double layer of heavy-duty aluminum foil. Place in a large dish or pan. Weigh it down with canned goods and refrigerate for 6 hours.

Remove pan from the refridgerator and drain off liquid. Turn the fish over, re-cover, and re-weight overnight. Next day, pour off any liquid that has developed. Repeat so that you have turned the fish twice and poured off the liquid 4 times.

On the day of serving, remove all spices, teas, and seasonings from the fish by wiping them off with a damp paper towel.

With a long, sharp knife, slice the salmon diagonally into very thin slices. Serve on a platter garnished with edible flowers, thinly sliced dark bread or pita toasts, and the lemon or lime wedges.

Prepare the Lime-Mustard Sauce only on the day it is to be served.

In a small bowl, blend lime juice into the mustard, sweetening to taste with brown sugar. Season with salt and pepper to taste. Whisk in the olive oil in a thin stream, then pour into a gravy boat or bowl for guests to use.

Rata-tea-ouille

The flavors of end-of-summer vegetables are enriched and lifted with a tea-based sauce. The classic Provençale assortment takes on an earthier taste when cooked in a fragrant Darjeeling bath, but other favorite teas from Assam or Nilgiri in India would work as well.

1 tablespoon/14 grams black Darjeeling tea leaves

3 cups/750 milliliters water

4 Japanese eggplants

2 medium tomatoes, peeled, seeded, and cubed

1 medium onion, chopped

1 medium zucchini, chopped

Salt and pepper to taste

Grated fresh ginger root to taste, about 1 tablespoon/14 grams

Optional: a pinch each of dried chili powder and sugar

Brew the tea in hot (190°F/88°C) water for about 3 minutes, then drain through a fine-meshed sieve, pressing hard on the tea leaves to extract as much of the infusion as possible. Set aside.

Char the eggplants on top of the stove or under the broiler if you have an electric stove. Butterfly by splitting them lengthwise, keeping both parts attached. Place in a baking pan and stuff with the tomatoes. Scatter the zucchini and onions over tomatoes and season with salt, pepper, and grated fresh ginger. Pour the brewed tea over all and bake uncovered at 350°F/177°C, basting occasionally. Cook for about 30 minutes, or until vegetables are tender. Add the chili powder and sugar as desired.

The resulting mélange of vegetables is blackish purple with patterns of light green zucchini and red tomato. Most of the sauce will be absorbed, but any remaining sauce can be reduced further to a glaze and poured over the dish. Serves 4 as a side dish for poultry or lamb or as a light luncheon dish served with rice and a salad.

Red Rice in Oolong Tea

This rice is worth seeking out for its nutty, chewy taste that is beautifully complemented by the rich, mouth-filling Wuyi Suixin, an incredible oolong from the Fujian region of mainland China. Other oolongs work equally well, such as a top-grade Formosa Oolong or Ti Kwan Yin, each contributing its own flavor character to the dish.

2 ½ tablespoons/35 grams Wuyi Suixin oolong tea leaves

4 cups/1 liter water

8 ounces/250 grams uncooked red rice, such as Colusari®

2 ounces/60 grams pecan halves

1 ounce/30 grams dried cherries or dried cranberries

1 bunch chives, finely chopped

Salt to taste

Steep the tea leaves in 4 cups/1 liter of hot (185°F/85°C) water. Pass leaves through a fine-meshed sieve and reserve liquid. Place the rice in a 2-quart/2-liter saucepan and add 3 cups/750 milliliters of the tea liquid to the pan, reserving the remaining 1 cup/240 milliliters of tea liquid. Bring to a boil then reduce to a simmer. Cover the pan and cook for about 25 to 30 minutes, or until rice tests done. This variety of rice will remain chewy and each kernel remains separate.

Toast pecans in a 350°F/177°C oven just until fragrant, about 5 minutes. Pour the additional cup of brewed tea into the finished rice to accentuate the tea flavor, cover, and allow to absorb. Garnish with a sprinkle of dried cherries or dried cranberries, the toasted pecans, and the chopped chives. Salt, as necessary, to taste.

This is a perfect accompaniment to our Sassy Bass with Aromatic Rub (page 72), Smoked Salmon Filets with Lapsang Souchong Cream Sauce (page 74), or Pan-Marinated Chicken with Smoked Tea (page 68). Or use it as the bed for any variety of lightly steamed or grilled seasonal vegetables. Yields 4 ample portions.

Smoked Chicken Salad with Tea Vinaigrette

Here a boldly flavored Chinese Yunnan tea is used in an oil-free dressing to add depth of flavor to this main dish salad. Water chestnuts add crunch and the ripe pears and dried currants provide a sweet counterpoint to the smokiness of the chicken. For a brief moment in late summer or early fall, fresh tiny champagne grapes are available. They make an elegant touch to this dish, or use the dried currants as noted. Great for lunch or a light supper.

Tea Dressing

1 cup/250 milliliters apple juice

1 tablespoon/14 grams Yunnan black tea leaves

1 teaspoon/5 milliliters Dijon-style mustard

1/2 cup/120 milliliters buttermilk

Salt and freshly ground black pepper to taste

For the Salad

1 pound/500 grams smoked chicken breasts (store-bought or you can smoke your own per the instructions on page 35)

1 cup/140 grams water chestnuts, well drained and sliced

2 ripe but firm Bosc pears (or other firm variety), peeled, then slivered

1 cup/140 grams dried currents, soaked in hot water or tea for five minutes and then drained

1 head of butter lettuce, washed and dried well, or 1 small head of Napa cabbage, thinly sliced

Bring the apple juice to a boil. Add the tea leaves and let steep for about 5 minutes. Strain through a fine-meshed sieve and place in a bowl. Cool. Blend the mustard and buttermilk, and then gradually add the cooled apple juice–infused tea. Add salt and pepper to taste. (A generous amount of black pepper is a nice added touch.)

Slice the chicken into long thin strips. Combine with the water chestnuts, pears, and currants. Coat with half of the dressing. Place on a bed of butter lettuce or shredded Napa cabbage. Pour the remaining dressing over each salad and serve immediately. Yields 4 portions.

Spring Rolls with Thai Tea Sauce

Don't be put off by the long ingredient list. Once the marketing is done, the preparation is simple. These elegant and delicate cylinders of vegetables and seafood may be made in advance, covered with a damp towel, and refrigerated. Easier still on the cook, simply present the cooked filling and the spring roll wrappers separately, Vietnamese style, and allow each guest to assemble his or her own roll just before eating.

1 tablespoon/15 milliliters
    vegetable oil

1 large clove garlic, finely minced

1-inch/2.5 millimiters piece of
    fresh ginger root, peeled and
    finely minced

1 shallot, peeled and finely minced

1 carrot, finely shredded

1 cup/250 grams white cabbage,
    finely shredded

$1/2$ cup/100 grams jicama,
    peeled, rough fibrous layer
    removed, finely shredded

4 shiitake mushrooms, thinly sliced

$1/4$ pound/60 grams sea scallops,
    cut into 1/2-inch cubes

$1/4$ pound/60 grams peeled and
    deveined shrimp, roughly chopped

1 tablespoon/15 milliliters reduced-
    sodium soy sauce

1 teaspoon/5 milliliters fish
    sauce, either Vietnamese
    (called nuoc nam) or Thai
    (called nam pla)

Freshly ground black pepper to taste

Chile powder to taste

12 rice paper wrappers

Prepare the filling: In a large heavy skillet, heat the oil just until hot. Add the garlic, ginger root, and shallot and sauté until softened but not browned. Add the carrot, cabbage, jicama, and mushrooms and sauté until wilted. Add the scallops and shrimp and sauté until they are firm, about 1 minute. Add the soy sauce, fish sauce, black pepper, and chile powder. Then stir to combine. Set aside to cool.

Prepare the Thai Tea Sauce: Thai tea is generally a finely powdered black tea flavored with vanilla and anise. If you can't find Thai tea in your favorite tea shop or ethnic market, bring finely powdered black tea and water to just under a boil. Over a heatproof bowl, pass through a fine-meshed sieve and return liquid to a clean saucepan. Add the vanilla bean, star anise, and sugar and simmer until the sugar is dissolved. If desired, sieve out solids and return to a clean saucepan to thicken by adding the dissolved cornstarch and bringing mixture to the boil. Remove from heat and serve at room temperature.

Assembly: In a shallow dish, place about $1/4$ inch/5 millimeters of cold water. Dip each rice paper wrapper briefly on each side just until moistened enough to be flexible. Place the wrapper on a flat surface and put a heaping tablespoon of the filling mixture on the center of the wrapper. Begin by folding in one side to enclose the mixture and then fold in each end tightly. Finish by rolling the packet compactly

Thai Tea Sauce

3 tablespoons/3 grams or 1¹/₂
ounces Thai tea leaves

1 cup/250 milliliters water

1 vanilla bean, split lengthwise to
expose its seeds

6 whole star anise

¹/₄ cup/50 grams sugar (or more
to taste)

Optional thickener: 1 table-
spoon/14 grams cornstarch dis-
solved in 2 tablespoons/30
milliliters cold water

to seal. Place on a platter seam side down and cover lightly with a dampened towel and then plastic wrap. Refrigerate.

When ready to serve, remove and allow to stand at room temperature. Serve with the tea sauce. Serves 6 as an appetizer, 4 as a light luncheon entrée.

Tea-Cured Salmon and Ginger Sandwich

*This elegant lunch or brunch dish is prepared from the Jasmine-Cured Salmon
(page 48), only without the Lime-Mustard Sauce. Thinly sliced tea-cured
salmon tops some rustic country bread. Steaming cups of malty Assam would
contrast sweetly with the bracing salmon. What a way to begin a leisurely
weekend morning. This is easy to assemble and tastes divine; you may never
opt for bagels and lox again!*

**8 thin slices of rustic bread (whole
grain, sourdough, or French)**

**1/2 cup/120 milliliters plain
yogurt, drained**

**1 small jicama, peeled, fibrous outer
layer removed, thinly sliced; if
unavailable, use peeled and thinly
sliced tart apple**

**6 to 8 ounces/170 to 230 grams
Jasmine-Cured Salmon, sliced as
thinly as possible**

Coarse salt, to taste

Freshly ground black pepper

1 small jar pickled ginger, store-bought

**Garnish: A few sprigs of fresh dill, fra-
grant coarse sea salt**

note

*The marine freshness of tea-cured salmon
can only be improved upon with
a sprinkling of one of those wonderful
artisan-produced sea salts from France.
To add this elusive layer of flavor, it pays
to search your specialty food store for
these sals de mer.*

Assembly: Toast the bread lightly. Cool and spread thinly with drained
yogurt. Place slices of jicama on each of 4 slices of bread. Drape 1/4 of
the salmon over jicama. Divide ginger and top salmon with it. Lightly
sprinkle salt and pepper over salmon, then finish the sandwiches with
the remaining slices of bread. Garnish with dill and coarse salt as
desired. Serves 4.

For a more elegant presentation, these look inviting as open-faced
sandwiches and require only 4 slices of bread. For heartier appetites,
serve 2 open-faced sandwiches per person, using 8 slices of bread.
Just before serving, sprinkle with fragrant coarse sea salt.

Pickling your own ginger

If you can't find pickled ginger at your supermarket, don't despair;
it's easy to prepare.

Bring 1/2 cup/125 milliliters of vinegar and 1/2 cup/100
grams sugar to a boil in a small saucepan. Slice and peel a 4-inch/
10-centimeter piece of ginger root; add it to the saucepan and simmer
until tender. Remove from heat and allow to cool. Store in a tightly
covered glass container, refrigerated, until ready to use. Leftovers
keep well and would add spark to a dressing for chicken or tuna salad.

Tea-Poached Plums

This elegant dish offers a double punch: use it as a piquant accompaniment to roasted meats or poultry, or serve it as a dessert with a creamy blue cheese or as a sweet/tart topping for ice cream or with shortbread. The vinegar provides the right counterpoint to the sweetness of the fruit. Forgiving Chinese Keemun tea is used as the main element for the sweetly spiced poaching liquid.

4 tablespoon/2 ounces dry Keemun leaves, lightly packed

2 quarts/2 liters water

2 cups/400 grams granulated sugar

1/2 cup/100 grams brown sugar, tightly packed

1 tablespoon/3 grams whole cloves

2 cinnamon sticks

1 tablespoon/4 grams whole black peppercorns, slightly cracked in a mortar and pestle

1 cup/250 milliliters cider vinegar or unseasoned rice vinegar

4 pounds/2 kilograms whole, slightly underripe fresh plums like Santa Rosa red, about 12 to 16, depending on size

Brew the tea using sub-boiling water, about 190°F/88°C, and steep for 3 minutes. Pour the brewed tea through a fine-meshed sieve to remove the leaves. Pour liquid into a 2-quart/2-liter saucepan and add granulated sugar, brown sugar, spices, and vinegar. Gently place the plums into the mixture and simmer about 10 minutes, or until tender. Remove from the heat and cool in the liquid at room temperature.

Remove the plums gently and place in a bowl. Sieve the poaching liquid to remove the solids and discard them, then pour liquid over the plums. Cool, then refrigerate, covered, until ready to eat. Remove plums from refrigerator. To serve, slice neatly in half, remove the pits, and place on the plate as a side dish. Garnish with additional sauce. Two plums make a generous serving. Yields 6 to 8 servings.

Tea-Smoked Mushrooms

A slight smokiness achieved using a wok as a smoker makes this mélange of mushrooms the perfect topping for whole wheat pasta or thick Japanese ramen noodles. Make sure your exhaust fan in the kitchen is in good working condition since this cooking method can produce some smoke. See page 35 for other smoking directions.

For Smoking Mixture

½ cup/120 grams dry rice

½ cup/100 grams brown sugar

½ cup/50 grams black tea leaves of your choice, such as Yunnan, Assam, Kenya, or Keemun

2 tablespoons/8 grams whole black peppercorns, cracked with a mallet or metal meat pounder

1 tablespoon/3 grams whole coriander seeds

4 slices fresh ginger root

4 cinnamon sticks

1 bay leaf

1 teaspoon/3 grams whole cloves

For Mushrooms

½ pound/250 grams assorted mushrooms, washed and dried (suggestions are shiitake, chanterelles, portobello, brown cremini, or garden variety white, in proportions to your taste)

4 large cloves of garlic, finely chopped

Olive oil to coat mushrooms

Reduced-sodium soy sauce to taste, about 1 teaspoon/5 milliliters

Freshly ground black pepper

Garnish: Fresh chopped chives or thinly sliced scallion greens

Line a wok with foil and place the smoking mixture (rice, sugar, tea, peppercorns, coriander, ginger root, cinnamon, bay leaf, and cloves) in a mound in the center of the foil in the wok.

Quarter or halve mushrooms, depending on their size, to bite-size pieces and place in a bowl. Toss lightly to coat with the garlic, olive oil, and soy sauce. Grind a good dose of black pepper over them and mix lightly to distribute the pepper evenly.

Set a wire rack in the wok and place a tight-fitting lid on top of the wok. Heat wok over a high flame until wisps of smoke appear when you briefly lift the lid.

Reduce the flame to medium. Quickly place the mushrooms on the rack in the wok and replace cover. Smoke about 5 minutes, less if you prefer a less smoky taste.

Remove mushrooms and place into a bowl to let stand at room temperature. Adjust seasoning as needed with salt and pepper to taste.

Top cooked whole wheat pasta or ramen noodles with the mushrooms and sprinkle the dish with chopped chives or thinly sliced scallion greens. Serve immediately. Serves 4.

Tea-Wilted Greens with Summer Fruit and Goat Cheese

This salad is perfect for those times when you wish to put a light summer din-
ner on the table yet not stay in the kitchen too long. Any greens, like Napa cab-
bage, will do, but Asian bok choi, kale, or tatsoi lend themselves best to this
study in contrasts. A fruity China black tea, such as Keemun or Yunnan, stands
up well to the assertive flavor of the greens. Some crusty whole grain bread
and a bottle of sturdy red wine will round out the meal.

4 tablespoons/2 ounces dried China
*   black tea leaves (Keemun*
*   or Yunnan)*

1 cup/250 milliliters boiling water

Fruity olive oil for wilting the greens,
*   plus additional oil to drizzle over*
*   dish at serving time*

1 tablespoon/3 grams fresh ginger
*   root, finely chopped*

1 1/2 pounds/700 grams
*   assorted greens, tough stems*
*   or ribs removed*

Salt and freshly ground black pepper
*   to taste*

5 ounces/140 grams mild, soft goat
*   cheese, cut into cubes or rounds*

2 ripe nectarines, plums, or apricots,
*   pitted and cut into wedges*

Olive oil to drizzle

Warm 4 plates.

Roast the tea leaves in a heavy dry skillet just until aromatic, about 2 minutes. Do not burn. Remove from the heat and carefully add the boiling water. Steep for 1 minute and then pass through a fine-meshed sieve, reserving the liquid.

Heat the oil over medium heat, in a large, heavy skillet. Add the ginger and stir constantly until aromatic. Do not burn. Add the greens and cook until slightly wilted. Season with salt and pepper to taste. (There should be some liquid remaining.)

Assembly: Divide the greens among the 4 warmed plates. Arrange the goat cheese and fruit wedges as you like over the greens. Drizzle with olive oil and serve immediately. Serves 4.

Entrées

Brisket Braised in Tea with Root Vegetables

Cold Tea Noodles

Dusty, Dark, Tea-Sauced Turkey Thighs

Morocco-Darjeeling Halibut

Pan-Marinated Chicken with Smoked Tea

Pork Tenderloin Cameroon with Prune-Stuffed Apples

Sassy Bass with Aromatic Rub

Smoked Salmon Filets with Lapsang Souchong Cream Sauce

Tea-Basted Roasted Chicken

Tea-Marinated Grilled Tofu Steaks

Tea-Sauced Scallops with Orange, Soy, and Honey

Tea-Smoked Chicken Wraps

Tea "Smoked" Trout with Indian Salsa

Brisket Braised in Tea with Root Vegetables

This dish is great for entertaining. It is best made the day before serving for two reasons: First, any fat that rises to the top of the braising liquid may be skimmed off easily when cold, and second, the flavors of the tea and the vegetable components settle in and marry overnight, producing a mellow, multilayered taste profile.

2 1/4 pounds/1 kilogram lean brisket of beef

Salt and freshly ground pepper

Fruity olive oil, enough to coat the pan for searing

1/2 bunch celery, washed well and cut into 1/2-inch/1-centimeter diagonal slices

1 1/2 cups/250 grams thinly sliced yellow onions (1 large onion)

4 carrots, washed and cut into 1/2-inch/1-centimeter rounds

1 parsnip, peeled and cut into 1/2-inch/1-centimeter chunks

1 rutabaga, peeled and cut into 1/2-inch/1-centimeter chunks

4 cloves garlic, smashed then finely chopped

4 tablespoons/2 ounces Keemun tea leaves, plus 4 tablespoons/ 2 ounces additional Keemun tea leaves to finish the sauce

2 quarts/2 liters water

1/2 cup/100 grams packed brown sugar

1/2 cup/120 milliliters ketchup

Preheat the oven to 350°F/177°C. Salt and pepper the brisket and sear in hot olive oil in a heavy skillet until the surface is browned. Turn only once, after about 5 minutes. Place the brisket in a heavy roasting pan and scatter the vegetables over the meat.

Brew the 4 tablespoons/2 ounces of tea in cool (170°F/77°C) water for 30 minutes. Sieve out and discard the leaves. Combine the brewed tea, brown sugar, and ketchup in a bowl to dissolve all the ingredients thoroughly, then pour over the brisket. Cover the pan with a lid and place in the oven for 2 1/2 hours, or until tender. Cool, then refrigerate, preferably overnight.

The next day, skim off any fat that collects on the surface of the braising liquid. Pour the defatted liquid into a heavy saucepan and cook over high heat until it is reduced by half. Add 4 tablespoons/ 2 ounces of Keemun tea leaves and return the liquid to the boil. Remove from the heat immediately. Pour the liquid through a fine-meshed sieve to remove the leaves. Adjust seasonings in the sauce with salt and pepper to taste.

With a sharp carving knife, slice meat across the grain into thin slices. Place decoratively on the plate along with vegetables. Drizzle sauce over each portion. Serves 4 to 6 generously.

Cold Tea Noodles

This refreshing dish provides an easy way out of the kitchen on a sweltering day. Keep cool by cooking the noodles in tea the night before you serve the dish. Next day, assemble the short list of ingredients and dinner is on the table. Shichimi togarashi is a Japanese spice mixture, available at Asian markets.

2 quarts/2 liters water

1 tablespoon/14 grams Japanese Genmaicha green tea leaves

1 pound/500 grams Chinese water noodles or Japanese udon noodles

1 package (12 ounces/340 grams) firm tofu, well drained

1 package enoki mushrooms

1 package radish sprouts, washed and dried

1 bunch scallions, sliced into very thin rounds

1 small bunch cilantro leaves

Light soy sauce

Japanese sesame oil

Shichimi togarashi or freshly ground black pepper

Bring 2 quarts/2 liters of water to 180°F/82°C and add tea. Steep for 3 minutes and pour through a sieve. Reserve liquid for cooking the noodles.

Heat the reserved tea to a boil and add noodles. Cook for about 5 minutes, or until noodles are still somewhat al dente. Remove from heat and allow the noodles to remain in the liquid until cooled. Remove noodles from liquid and place in a bowl, covered, overnight in the refrigerator.

Next day, cover the tofu with several layers of paper toweling and place it on a plate. Press any excess moisture from the tofu by setting a 2-pound/1-kilogram weight (approximately) upon it. Remove weight and paper toweling after 15 minutes. Discard any liquid that has accumulated on the plate. Carefully slice the tofu into 1-inch/3-centimeter cubes and set aside.

Place equal amounts of noodles on each of 4 plates. Scatter tofu and remaining ingredients evenly over all. Serve with soy sauce, sesame oil, and seasoning as desired. Serves 4.

Dusty, Dark, Tea-Sauced Turkey Thighs

This dish spells fall or winter. Dark thigh meat, which cooks up moist and tender, is the cut of choice, but you may substitute the breast if your audience objects. Adjust cooking times accordingly, though, as dark meat takes a little longer than white. Any Assam or Kenya tea would complete the poultry. A jar of lingonberries, readily found in the grocery jam aisle, or fresh cranberries in season, lend a ruby glisten to the sauce. A baked winter squash would round out the plate.

2 pounds/1 kilogram turkey thighs, skin and all visible fat removed

Olive oil to coat meat lightly

Salt

Freshly ground black pepper

1 large onion, roughly chopped

1 large carrot, peeled and roughly chopped

1 large clove garlic, smashed and finely chopped

1 quart/1 liter vegetable stock or water

2 tablespoons/28 grams Assam tea leaves

1 bay leaf

$^1/_2$ teaspoon/2.4 grams dried thyme leaves

$^1/_4$ cup/60 milliliters full-bodied ruby port

8 ounces fresh cranberries or one 14-ounce jar lingonberries, well drained

Optional: granulated sugar to sweeten the sauce

Rub the turkey with olive oil then season with salt and pepper. In a heavy skillet, sear the turkey, turning occasionally to brown evenly. Remove the meat to a plate and pour off any fat that may have accumulated in the pan. Add the onion, carrot, and garlic and cook over medium heat, stirring until softened but not browned. Return the turkey to the pan.

Heat the vegetable stock or water until just under the boil. Add the tea leaves, bay leaf, and thyme to the vegetable stock or water and steep for about 5 minutes or until the tea leaves are fully unfurled. Pass through a fine-meshed sieve and pour over the turkey. Cook over medium heat, covered, for about 35 minutes, or until the meat is fully cooked. Remove the meat to a platter and keep warm, covered, in a 200°F/ 93°C oven.

Meanwhile, over high heat, reduce the cooking liquid by half. Add the port and the lingonberries (or cranberries) and simmer for about 5 minutes. Adjust seasonings. Add sugar to taste. Remove the turkey from the bone, if desired. To plate, pour a little of the sauce on the dish, top with the turkey, then mask the turkey with more sauce. Serve the remainder of the sauce on the side. Serves 4.

Morocco-Darjeeling Halibut

A sunny fusion of flavors from two places on the same latitude yet miles apart, India and Morocco, dominate the mild taste of the halibut. The sweet/hot spices are utterly delicious and the soft muscatel Darjeeling exquisitely balances this dish.

2-pounds/1 kilogram halibut steak, bone in, about 1 inch/3 centimeters thick

$^1/_2$ teaspoon/3 grams coarse salt

$^1/_2$ teaspoon/3 grams freshly ground black pepper

2 tablespoons/30 milliliters fruity olive oil

1 large onion, thinly sliced

1 pound/500 grams fresh red, ripe tomatoes, skinned and seeded, roughly chopped

1 large lemon, well washed, thinly sliced, seeds removed

1 cup/140 grams dark raisins

1 teaspoon/3 grams dried ground ginger

$^1/_2$ teaspoon/2 grams ground allspice

4 cloves garlic, smashed then finely minced

$^1/_2$ teaspoon/2 grams hot pepper powder (Moroccan, French piment d'Espelette, Hungarian hot paprika, Aleppo pepper, or Italian hot pepper flakes)

1 quart/1 liter spring water

4 tablespoons/2 ounces Darjeeling muscatel tea leaves

$^1/_2$ cup/115 milliliters lavender or clover honey (the more fragrant the better)

Wash and dry the fish. Season on both sides with salt and pepper. Lightly coat an ovenproof (oven to table) 3-quart/3-liter baking dish with olive oil. Center the fish, onions, and tomatoes in the dish. Scatter lemon slices and raisins over all. Add the remaining spices to the dish. Brew the tea in water heated to 185 to 190°F/85 to 88°C for 5 minutes, then dissolve the honey in it. Pour all of it over the fish and bake, covered lightly with foil, for about 35 minutes or until fish flakes easily when pierced with a fork.

Carefully pour the braising liquid from the pan into a heavy 2-quart/2-liter saucepan. Keep the fish warm, covered, in a 200°F/93°C oven while reducing the liquid over high heat to a coating consistency. Uncover just before serving to allow the diners to inhale the heavenly aroma wafting from the dish. Divide the fish into 4 equal pieces and sauce each. Perfect accompaniments are steamed butternut squash lightly seasoned with cinnamon and fragrant basmati rice. Serves 4.

Pan-Marinated Chicken with Smoked Tea

Humble and healthful white meat chicken is given a new dimension cooked in a mixture of brewed tea and fresh ginger root. The best tea to use is a very smoky Lapsang Souchong, which is further, and boldly, flavored with fresh ginger.

2 cups/500 milliliters water

2 tablespoons/28 grams Lapsang Souchong tea leaves

3-inch/7-centimeter piece of fresh ginger root, peeled and sliced thinly into rounds

4 chicken breasts, boneless, skin removed

2 teaspoons plus 1 tablespoon/ 25 milliliters fruity olive oil

2 cloves garlic, finely chopped

2 medium onions, finely chopped

2 carrots, diced

2 stalks celery, diced

2 leeks, white part only, well washed and finely chopped

Salt and freshly ground black pepper

1 pound/500 grams fresh spinach (or other fresh greens such as chard) stems removed, well washed and dried

Bring 2 cups/500 milliliters of water to a boil. Cool for 5 minutes and then add tea leaves. Let steep for 3 minutes and then sieve to remove tea leaves. Add the ginger root rounds and place the chicken breasts into the liquid. Marinate for 1 hour, refrigerated.

In a heavy sauté pan, heat 2 teaspoons/10 milliliters of olive oil until hot. Remove chicken from marinade, drain, and dry, then cook briefly, just until surface is golden brown (the chicken should remain un-cooked in the middle since it will be cooked thoroughly in the tea marinade). Remove chicken from pan and set aside.

Add the garlic to the sauté pan, stirring constantly until it releases its flavor but does not brown, about 20 seconds. Add onion, carrots, celery, and leeks and cover over low heat just until tender but not browned.

Add the chicken and tea marinade to the cooked vegetables in the pan and cook over low heat, covered, for about 10 to 15 minutes, or until the chicken is just firm to the touch and no longer pink. During the cooking, do not allow the liquid to come to a boil at any point. When the chicken is done, remove pan from heat and cool at room tempera-ture, then remove chicken from the pan and set aside, covered.

Purée the vegetables and cooking liquid in a blender or food processor until smooth. Add salt and pepper to taste. Set sauce aside.

For final assembly: Heat 1 tablespoon/15 milliliters of olive oil in a sauté pan and add spinach. Cook just to wilt, then reserve. Slice chicken on the diagonal into $\frac{1}{2}$-inch/1-centimeter strips. On each plate, center a mound of spinach and top with the chicken. Spoon a ring of sauce around the spinach and chicken and serve any remaining sauce as desired. Serves 4.

Pork Tenderloin Cameroon with Prune-Stuffed Apples

Tea from Cameroon is grown on the hills surrounding Mount Cameroon, West Africa's only active volcano. Sweet, with a chocolate edge, Cameroon tea is the basis for the haunting sauce of this dish. Feel free to reduce the brown sugar if you favor a less sweet sauce.

4 tablespoons/2 ounces Cameroon tea leaves

1 quart/1 liter boiling water

2 cups/500 milliliters unsweetened apple juice (or fresh apple cider if available)

2 pounds/1 kilogram pork tenderloin (2 pieces)

Salt and freshly ground black pepper

1 tablespoon/8 grams dry mustard powder

1/2 cup/100 grams brown sugar

2 tablespoons/30 milliliters fruity olive oil

6 medium Golden Delicious apples, peeled and cored

12 pitted prunes

Cornstarch as needed, to thicken the sauce

Garnish: chopped chives

Preheat oven to 350°F/177°C. Brew the tea in the water and steep for about 2 minutes. Using a fine-meshed sieve, strain out the tea leaves, reserving the liquid. Combine the tea with the apple juice and set aside.

Salt and pepper the pork (be generous with the pepper). Mix the mustard powder and brown sugar together, making sure that the mixture has no lumps. Add 1 tablespoon of the reserved tea liquid to moisten, then spread out on a flat surface and coat the meat. Heat a heavy sauté pan until very hot, then add the oil and heat until oil is hot. Carefully place the meat in the pan and sear over medium-high heat to brown, about 7 to 10 minutes in all, turning as necessary to brown evenly. Remove pan from heat. Peel and core the apples, then slice them horizontally. Put them back together neatly and stuff them with the prunes.

Place the meat into a 10x12-inch/25x30-centimeter nonstick roasting pan and pour the tea-juice liquid over the meat. Surround the meat with the stuffed apples and bake in the oven for 45 minutes to 1 hour, basting the meat and apples occasionally. When done, the meat should register 165°F/74°C on a meat thermometer.

Remove from the oven and carefully pour off cooking liquid into another saucepan. Keep the meat and apples warm, covered, in a 200°F/93°C oven.

Reduce the cooking liquid by half by heating over high heat until it lightly coats a spoon, about 5 to 7 minutes. Add a little cornstarch to thicken. Taste to adjust seasoning.

Slice the meat in $1/2$-inch/1.5-centimeter rounds, and mask with the sauce. Garnish each plate with an apple and a few chives, if desired, and serve immediately. Place remaining sauce in a heated gravy boat. Yields 6 servings.

Sassy Bass with Aromatic Rub
(see recipe for Oolong Rice, page 50)

In this dish, Kanyam Golden tea from Nepal, grown high in the Himalayas, lends its Darjeeling personality to an aromatic spice rub. Highly forgiving, this tea has an aromatic, floral essence that is a suitable match for the highly spiced rub. Use thick center cuts of white-fleshed fish such as Mexican sea bass, Pacific red snapper, striped bass, or cod. Starting with whole spices and reducing them to a powder along with the tea leaves yields a remarkable fragrance.

4 tablespoons/2 ounces Kanyam Golden
   Nepal tea leaves

$1/2$ teaspoon/2 grams ground ginger

1 cinnamon stick

$1/2$ teaspoon/1 gram whole
   coriander seeds

$1/4$ teaspoon/1 gram whole black
   peppercorns

1 tablespoon/13 grams brown sugar

$1/2$ teaspoon/2 grams salt

Olive oil to rub on fish

1 $1/2$ pounds/680 grams fish, cut into
   $3/4$-inch/2-centimeter filets

Garnish: 12 sprigs cilantro (coriander)

Spicy Mango Salsa

1 ripe mango, peeled and
   roughly chopped

1 small cucumber, peeled,
   seeded, and cut into
   $1/4$-inch/.5-centimeter dice

Enough freshly squeezed orange
   juice just to moisten the salsa,
   about $1/4$ cup/60 milliliters

1 tablespoon/13 grams
   brown sugar

Chili paste to taste

Salt to taste

Thin Tea Sauce

1 cup/250 milliliters vegetable stock

1 teaspoon/5 grams Kanyam
   Golden Nepal tea

In an electric spice grinder or using a mortar and pestle, process the first seven ingredients until a fine powder results. Spread out on a plate and set aside.

Rub the fish with olive oil on both sides to coat lightly. Dip fish into the spice rub, coating well on both sides. Let the fish rest at room temperature about 15 minutes for spices to penetrate the flesh of the fish and make the delicious "crust."

Preheat the oven to 425°F/218°C. Heat a cast-iron skillet until almost white hot (a drop of water placed in the pan will evaporate almost instantly when the pan is sufficiently hot). Reduce heat under the pan to medium and place the fish carefully into the pan. Cook for about 5 minutes on each side, turning once, then finish cooking in the oven for about 10 minutes. Do not overcook.

Spicy Mango Salsa

Combine all the ingredients in a small bowl and keep at room temperature to allow the flavors to mingle well, at least 5 minutes before serving. Can be refrigerated up to 2 days.

Thin Tea Sauce

Gently heat the stock to just under a boil, about 185°F/85°C. Add tea leaves and brew 2 minutes. Sieve out leaves completely, pressing down to get all the tea liquor.

To assemble this dish, spoon out Thin Tea Sauce on each of 4 plates. Place a piece of fish on top of the sauce, then spoon Spicy Mango Salsa on top of the fish. Garnish with several sprigs of cilantro. Serve extra sauce on the side. Yields 4 servings.

Smoked Salmon Filets with Lapsang Souchong Cream Sauce

The sweet taste of smoking and the classic earthiness of Lapsang Souchong blend seamlessly in this fish recipe for all seasons. The result is a complexly flavored dish in a soft palette of colors: the pale celadon of the sage leaves and artichoke hearts against the blush of coral from the salmon.

2 to 2 1/2 pounds/1 kilogram (approximately) side of filet of fresh salmon

Salt and white pepper to taste

1 tablespoon/3 grams dried thyme

1 tablespoon/15 milliliters olive oil

2 tablespoons/28 grams Lapsang Souchong tea leaves

2 cups/500 milliliters water

2 cups/500 milliliters vegetable or fish stock

1 cup/250 milliliters crème fraîche

6 large (or 12 small) water-packed artichoke hearts (fresh artichoke hearts can be used by blanching them in salted water for about 5 minutes or until tender)

2 to 3 fresh sage leaves

Salt and pepper the salmon and cut into 6 pieces. This recipe uses two different techniques to cook the salmon. First, we use the smoking mixture noted on page 35, adding the thyme to augment the seasoning slightly. Smoke the salmon in a wok for about 5 minutes, then remove from the pan and set aside. Next, heat the olive oil in a heavy, large pan until almost smoking. Place the salmon in the pan skin side down and cover. Pan-broil the fish to seal in the juices, about 10 to 15 minutes, depending on the thickness of the filet. Remove to a warm platter to rest.

Brew the tea in hot water (about 195°F/91°C) for about 3 minutes. Then add the vegetable stock to the tea and heat thoroughly. (If using canned stock, reduce salt in the recipe.)

Skim the fat off the bottom of the pan, then add the tea and stock mixture to deglaze the pan. Reduce the liquid to half, then add the crème fraîche and reduce the sauce further by 1/3. (Crème fraîche does not curdle like heavy cream can.) Add the fresh sage leaves and artichokes and cook only to heat them through, about 1 minute. Adjust the seasoning as necessary.

Mask each plate with the sauce, then place a piece of salmon gently in the center of the plate and garnish lightly with additional sauce. Place an artichoke on the side and serve immediately. Serves 6.

For an alternative, lower-fat version, though no less luxurious, use the following sauce:

4 scallions, trimmed to include three inches of the green tops

3-inch/7-centimeter piece of fresh ginger root, peeled and roughly chopped

¹/₂ cup/120 milliliters low-sodium soy sauce

2 teaspoons/8 grams brown sugar

1 large clove garlic, peeled and crushed

2 tablespoons/28 grams Lapsang Souchong tea leaves

Process all of the ingredients in a blender or food processor until smooth. Over a small bowl, pass the mixture through a fine-meshed sieve, pressing hard on the solids to extract the liquid. Transfer to a heavy 1-quart/1-liter saucepan and reduce the liquid over high heat just until the sauce coats a spoon lightly. Do not burn. If you have reduced too much, add a bit of hot water to thin slightly. Drizzle over the salmon and serve.

Tea-Basted Roasted Chicken

The charm of this dish is its simplicity. What could be better than a chicken roasted to perfection, golden brown and crisp-skinned, paired with a dusky, dark, tea-based sauce? The sauce takes its inspiration from the yak-buttered tea of Tibet, but in this case the tea is Chinese and the butter is the American variety. No matter where you are, you can enjoy this dish, infused with the aura of the steppes of central Asia.

1 quart/1 liter water

1/2 cup/100 grams Keemun tea leaves

2-inch/5-centimeter piece of ginger root, peeled and sliced into coins

6 cloves garlic, peeled then crushed to release their aroma

1 cup/250 milliliters vegetable stock (homemade or canned will do)

Olive oil to coat roasting pan and to brush on chicken before roasting

1 large whole roasting chicken (2 to 3 pounds/1 to 1.5 kilograms), well washed and dried

Salt and freshly ground black pepper

1 teaspoon/4 grams granulated sugar or to taste

2 ounces/60 grams unsalted (sweet) butter

Bring the water to a boil. Add the tea leaves and infuse for 3 minutes. Strain through a fine-meshed sieve into a bowl, extracting as much liquid as possible, then pour into a clean saucepan. Add ginger, garlic, and vegetable stock and return liquid to a boil. Remove from heat, sieve out and discard the solids, and reserve liquid.

Preheat the oven to 450°F/232°C. Brush a heavy 12-inch/30-centimeter skillet lightly with olive oil. Salt and pepper the chicken inside and out. Place chicken into heavy skillet and pour about 1/2 cup/120 milliliters of the brewed tea over it. Roast for about an hour until juices run clear, basting with tea mixture every 20 minutes or so. Test chicken with a meat thermometer; at 170°F/77°C, it is done. Skim the fat from the liquid in the pan. Remove chicken to a cutting board, carve into 8 pieces, and place on a platter to keep warm. Reduce the basting liquid to coating consistency, adjusting the seasoning to taste. This dish is even more delicious with a generous grind of black pepper. Add sugar to taste.

Off heat, add butter to the reduced liquid in small bits, whisking until blended. Strain sauce through a fine-meshed sieve and pour into a heated sauceboat. Serve immediately. We suggest such accompaniments as wild rice, sautéed portobello mushrooms, and curly (Savoy) cabbage, as desired. Serves 4.

Tea-Marinated Grilled Tofu Steaks

In homage to new-wave Japanese fare and the public hunger for more meaning-ful exchanges with tofu on the plate, this dish uses delicate chanterelles instead of dried bonito flakes (katsuobushi) *which top the original version. And instead of drinking green tea with the dish as one might in a Japanese restau-rant, we use Yunnan, a black Chinese tea, as both marinade and base for the sauce.*

14 ounces/400 grams of firm tofu, well drained

2 teaspoons/10 grams Yunnan tea leaves

1 quart/1 liter water

1 teaspoon/10 milliliters light soy sauce

1 large garlic clove, crushed, plus 1 large garlic clove, finely minced for the mushrooms

2-inch/5-centimeter piece of fresh ginger root, peeled and thinly sliced

1 tablespoon/14 grams brown sugar

2 teaspoons/10 milliliters olive oil for tofu plus 1 teaspoon/5 milliliters for mushrooms

2 ounces/60 grams fresh chanterelles or other mushrooms (shiitake, oyster, or any combination you choose)

Slice tofu horizontally into 2 rectangles of equal thickness. To extract the excess liquid, wrap tofu in several sheets of paper towels and place on a sheet pan. Set a 1-pound/.5-kilogram weight on another sheet pan and place it on top of the tofu in the first pan for about a half hour. This may be done in advance with the tofu stored in the refrigerator until ready to cook.

Brew the tea leaves in 1 quart/1 liter of sub-boiling water, about 195° F/91°C, and steep 3 minutes. Pour the brewed tea through a fine-meshed sieve to remove the leaves. Using a bowl large enough to accommodate the tofu without crushing it, place the tea into a com-bination of the soy sauce, garlic, ginger root, and brown sugar. Gently place the tofu in the liquid and marinate for at least 1 hour at cool room temperature or overnight in the refrigerator.

Clean and dry the mushrooms and set aside.

Remove tofu from the marinade, reserve the liquid. Dry the tofu well with paper towels. Heat a heavy skillet until hot. Add the oil and then carefully place the tofu into the pan. Be careful, as the oil may spat-ter. Cook for 5 minutes, then turn and cook for another 5 minutes, or until golden brown. Remove from pan and keep warm while you cook the mushrooms.

Heat 1 teaspoon/5 milliliters of olive oil in a heavy skillet. Add the garlic and mushrooms and cook, moving mushrooms gently until

golden brown. Remove from heat and reserve. Reduce the marinade in a heavy saucepan until thick enough to lightly coat a spoon. Add mushrooms and toss to coat with the sauce. Taste to adjust seasonings as necessary.

Place tofu on warmed plates. Top with sauced mushrooms and drizzle remaining sauce over all. Serves 4 as an appetizer or small first course.

Tea-Sauced Scallops with Orange, Soy, and Honey

The sweetness of large fresh scallops blends beautifully with the fruity character of Chinese black Keemun tea and sweet-tart orange. Cooked quickly, the scallops retain their juice and tenderness. A side of Chinese water noodles or al dente pasta rounds out the plate and provides a perfect nest for the scallops. Great for summer when you want to get out of the kitchen fast.

2 tablespoons/60 milliliters fruity olive oil

1 large clove garlic

1 pound/500 grams sea scallops

Juice of 1 large orange (about ¹/₂ cup/120 milliliters)

1 tablespoon/14 grams Keemun tea leaves

2 teaspoons/10 milliliters light soy sauce

1 tablespoon/5 milliliters honey

Cooked Chinese noodles or linguine pasta

Garnish: Fresh cilantro leaves or finely slivered green part of a scallion

Heat the olive oil until hot, almost smoking. Add the garlic and stir briefly. Next add the scallops and cook 2 minutes on each side, turning once to brown evenly. Remove the scallops to a small bowl and cover to keep warm while making the sauce.

Deglaze the pan with the orange juice, stirring to dislodge any browned particles that adhere to the pan. Add the tea leaves and cook, stirring for another 30 seconds. Add the soy sauce, honey, and any liquid from the scallops that has pooled in the bowl. Cook just until the sauce thickens slightly.

Pour through a fine-meshed sieve placed over a bowl and return sauce to the pan. Taste to correct seasoning if necessary. Coat the scallops with the sauce and serve in a nest of noodles or pasta. Garnish with cilantro or scallion as desired. Serves 4.

Tea-Smoked Chicken Wraps

(see recipe for Darjeeling Peach Conserve, page 42)

This is wonderful picnic fare, a colorful mosaic of white meat chicken, green lettuce, and red pepper, tidily arranged in a thin envelope of Middle Eastern flat bread. With a supply of tea-smoked chicken breasts and the peach conserve on hand, completing this rolled sandwich takes no time at all. Lavash is an unleavened cracker bread, sold in Middle Eastern or whole-food markets.

1 head romaine lettuce

1 medium red pepper

¼ cup/60 milliliters reduced-sodium soy sauce

½ cup/100 grams brown sugar

2 pounds/1 kilogram skinless, boneless chicken breasts, all visible fat removed (bone-in chicken can be used but requires longer cooking time, up to 30 minutes)

1 bunch fresh arugula or watercress, leaves only, stems removed, washed and dried

¼ cup/60 milliliters mayonnaise

Salt and freshly ground black pepper to taste

2 sheets of lavash bread, edges cut to form 2 circular halves, each 13"x23"

Wash the romaine well, dry, then remove and discard the core. Separate each leaf and cut out the heavy ribs, then shred and set aside. Seed the red pepper and slice thinly into long julienne strips. Combine the soy sauce with the sugar, making sure to dissolve all the sugar.

Remove all visible fat from the chicken and marinate in the soy and brown sugar for an hour, or longer, in the refrigerator.

Combine the arugula and mayonnaise in a blender or food processor until smooth. Refrigerate, covered, until ready to use.

To smoke the chicken, you will need a wok, a rack that will fit into it as a surface for the food being smoked, and a tight-fitting lid for the wok.

Line the wok with foil, then place the smoking mixture in a mound in the center of the foil. Place the cover on the wok and heat the wok over a high flame until wisps of smoke appear when you briefly lift the lid to take a peek. Reduce the flame to medium. Set the rack into the wok.

Using tongs, quickly place the chicken onto the rack in the wok and cover tightly. Smoke for about 10 minutes, or until the chicken is done. It should feel springy to the touch and register 165°F/74°C on an instant-read thermometer.

Smoking Mixture

$^1/_2$ *cup/100 grams dry uncooked rice*

$^1/_2$ *cup/100 grams brown sugar*

$^1/_2$ *cup/100 grams black tea leaves such as Assam, Kenya, Ceylon, or Yunnan*

2 tablespoons/6 grams whole black peppercorns, cracked with a mallet or metal meat pounder

1 tablespoon/3 grams whole coriander seeds

4 slices fresh ginger root

4 cinnamon sticks

1 bay leaf

1 teaspoon/2 grams whole cloves

1 apple, sliced into eighths

1 orange, sliced into eighths

Place the cooked chicken in a bowl and let stand at room temperature. When cooled, slice chicken into long strips. Adjust seasoning as needed with salt and pepper to taste. (Chicken breasts can be refrigerated at this point if you want to use them later.)

To prepare the wraps, place one lavash sheet on a work table. Spray the lavash sheet lightly with water, just to moisten. Repeat with the second sheet of lavash, stacking it on top of the first one. With a spatula or wide knife, spread the arugula mayonnaise in an even layer on the top sheet, including the edges. Salt and pepper to taste.

Place half the shredded romaine in a line parallel to the long side of the lavash 4 inches/10 centimeters in from the outside of the long edge toward the center. Place strips of red pepper on top of the romaine, then top the red pepper with the chicken. Top the chicken with the remaining romaine.

Fold in the short sides of the lavash, then roll it lengthwise tightly over the filling and the end folds. Create a tight, round log shape, like a jelly roll, and continue to roll until the lavash fully encloses the filling.

Spray the lavash again lightly with water and cover tightly with plastic wrap. Refrigerate until serving. Remove from the refrigerator a few minutes before serving to allow the wraps to lose some of their chill and enhance the flavor.

If serving immediately, store in the plastic wrap only for about 5 minutes at room temperature to allow the lavash to soften slightly. Cut and serve. Slice the rolls on the diagonal to show off the colors of the filling. Serve with Darjeeling Peach Conserve (page 42). Yields 12 to 16 wrapped sandwiches, each about 2$^1/_2$ to 3 inches/6 to 7.5 centimeters in diameter and $^3/_4$ inch/1.5 centimeters thick.

Tea "Smoked" Trout with Indian Salsa

With its delicate, dense flesh, trout is a perfect fish for this poached-in-smoky-tea treatment. A raft of slow-cooked, caramelized onions blankets each portion and an Indian-style raita of cucumbers and tomatoes in yogurt adds a bit of summer on the plate.

Cucumber-Tomato Raita

1 cup/250 milliliters plain yogurt, well drained (whole milk yogurt is best, but you may substitute either the lowfat or nonfat version if you wish)

1 teaspoon/2 grams cumin seeds

1 English cucumber or regular cucumber, peeled with seeds removed, thinly sliced

1 large red, ripe tomato (peeled and seeded), sliced into long strips (about 1 cup)

Salt to taste

1 teaspoon/4 grams granulated sugar

Freshly ground black pepper

Drain the yogurt in cheesecloth or a fine-meshed sieve set over a bowl to eliminate excess moisture. Roast the cumin seeds in a heavy skillet over medium heat, stirring constantly, until they release their aroma. Watch closely, as these burn easily. Grind seeds in an electric spice grinder or with a mortar and pestle. Set aside.

Combine the cucumber and tomato with salt to taste. Add the cumin and sugar and mix to blend. Add the yogurt and black pepper to taste and set aside at room temperature. (This may be prepared earlier in the day and refrigerated. Excess liquid may need to be drained before serving.)

In a heavy sauté pan, cook the onions in the olive oil over low heat until softened and golden brown. Stir occasionally. Do not allow these to burn. Set aside.

Brew the tea leaves in hot (185°F/85°C) water for 2 to 4 minutes, then sieve out the leaves immediately. Return the brewed tea to a saucepan large enough to accommodate the trout filets in a single layer. Add the celery, salt, brown sugar, and garlic; place the fish in the pan and cover tightly. Bring to a simmer and cook for about 10 minutes, or until fish is firm to the touch.

Pour off the cooking liquid into a heavy saucepan and cook over high heat to reduce by half. The sauce should lightly coat a spoon. Meanwhile, keep the fish and celery warm, covered, in a 200°F/93°C

For the fish:

1 medium onion, thinly sliced

*2 tablespoons/30 milliliters fruity
extra virgin olive oil*

*4 tablespoons/56 grams Lapsang
Souchong tea leaves*

1½ quarts/1.5 liters water

*2 pounds/1 kilogram (6 filets) of
trout, skin removed*

*½ bunch celery, well washed,
thinly sliced in diagonal cuts*

½ teaspoon/3 grams salt

*1 tablespoon/13 grams
brown sugar*

*2 cloves garlic, peeled then
smashed*

oven until ready to serve. Assembly: Warm 4 dinner plates. Place an equal amount of celery on each plate, then place equal portions of the fish on top of the celery. Coat each piece with the caramelized onions. Drizzle the reduced poaching liquid over each portion. Serve the Cucumber Tomato-Raita on the side. Serves 4.

Desserts

Awesome Assam Lemon Tart

Broiled Tea-Glazed Oranges with Flan Thé

Chai Ice Cream

Chai Ros Malai (Quick "Indian" Cream in Masala Chai)

Chai Scones

Chocolate Melting Moments Torte with Tea Crème Anglaise

Earl Grey Truffles

Fresh Peach-Darjeeling Sorbet

Green Tea–Poached Asian Pears with Pistachio Cream Sauce

Grilled Pineapple with Vanilla Tea-Crème Anglaise

Honeydew Green Tea Frappe

Milk Chocolate Torte with Assam Tea Ganache

Jasmine-Lemongrass Tea Sorbet

Peaches in Kenya Tea Sauce

Real Green Tea Ice Cream with Sesame-Caramel Sauce

Snowy Silver Needle Sorbet

White Chocolate Mousse with Bitter Lime Sauce

Awesome Assam Lemon Tart

Taking advantage of the mellow, almost creamy character of Assam, the filling for this tart acquires its attractive butterscotch color from the reddish hue of the tea, which has been steeped not in water but in fresh lemon juice. (Note: Be aware that this filling is designed to be meltingly soft; if you wish a firmer, sweeter final product, reduce the lemon juice to 6 tablespoons.)

The short dough can be used for both the crust and shortbread cookies. Shape into a ½ -inch/1-centimeter round disc sprinkled with granulated sugar, scored into wedges. Bake at 325°F/163°C for about 35 to 45 minutes, or until golden brown. For neat triangles, cut on the score marks as soon as the short-bread comes out of the oven. Warning: These are irresistible when warm.

Dough Ingredients

½ pound/230 grams unsalted (sweet) butter at room temperature

¼ cup/50 grams granulated white sugar

Zest of ½ lemon, yellow part only (the white pith can be bitter, so avoid grating it along with the zest)

1 whole large egg

¾ cup/150 grams all-purpose flour

Using the bowl of an electric mixer or a food processor with the steel knife attachment, cream the butter until soft and fluffy. Add the sugar and zest and mix to blend. In a small bowl, break the egg and stir lightly. Process briefly to blend it into the mix. Add flour and process just until the flour disappears. Remove from the mixer or processor bowl and place on a lightly floured surface. Knead briefly and flatten into a disc, about ½-inch/1-centimeter thick. Wrap and refrigerate until firm. While the dough is chilling, make the curd.

In a small, nonreactive saucepan, bring the lemon juice and tea leaves to a boil. Remove from heat and steep only for 1 minute. Sieve the mixture into a small bowl, pressing hard on the tea leaves to extract as much of the liquid as possible. Reserve the liquid but discard the leaves.

In a 3-quart/3-liter saucepan, bring 3 inches/7.5 centimeters of water to a boil. Place the sieved liquid plus the lemon zest, eggs, egg yolks, sugar, and butter into a stainless steel bowl large enough to fit snugly over the saucepan, acting as a double boiler. Note: This technique is preferable to an actual double boiler because there is more

Tea and Lemon Curd Filling

*¹/₂ cup/120 milliliters freshly
squeezed lemon juice*

*4 tablespoons/56 grams Assam
tea leaves*

Zest of 1 lemon

*2 whole large eggs plus 2 egg yolks
from large eggs*

*³/₄ cup/150 grams granulated
white sugar*

*¹/₄ pound/115 grams unsalted
(sweet) butter*

*Garnishes (optional): Natural,
unsalted pistachio nuts, finely
chopped; crystallized ginger,
thinly sliced; or candied
lemon slices*

room in which to whisk the ingredients vigorously, thus eliminating a mixture that ends up stiff, not altogether mixed, or burnt as a result of the pesky corners of a traditional double boiler.

Reduce the heat to medium so that the water is just simmering. Whisk constantly until the mixture is the thickness of mayonnaise, making sure to scrape the mixture well from the sides of the bowl. Put the mixture through a fine-meshed sieve to remove any lumps and set aside to cool to room temperature.

Remove the dough from the refrigerator. On a lightly floured surface, roll dough to a 14-inch/35-centimeter round about ¹/₄-inch/6 millimeters thick. Slide a metal spatula under the dough to make sure it is not sticking to the rolling surface. Roll up over the rolling pin and ease into an 8-inch-/20-centimeter-diameter, false-bottomed tart pan, pressing the dough firmly into the fluted sides of the pan. Prick with a fork at 1-inch/2-centimeter intervals all around the base of the tart.

Chill until frozen, about 30 minutes. Using the remaining dough, prepare the shortbread as noted above.

While the dough is in the freezer, preheat oven to 400°F/204°C.

Remove tart pan from freezer and bake on middle rack of oven for about 35 minutes, or until golden brown. Cool. Spread filling evenly in a ¹/₂-inch/1-centimeter layer and decorate with the garnishes of your choice. Serve at room temperature. Yields 6 servings.

Note: The recipe provides enough dough for both the tart and about 20 shortbread triangles. (One can never have enough shortbread.)

Broiled Tea-Glazed Oranges with Flan Thé

This recipe is actually two desserts in one, but they make such a winning combination we couldn't resist showing them together. The dense, rich taste of the flan is thanks to the cream cheese, which supplements the usual milk and cream found in most flans. The sweet, creamy taste of the flan is beautifully balanced with the tangy oranges, and each recipe has the distinct fruity character of a tea-infusion to provide that extra something that separates this dish from the ordinary.

The flan uses the floral muscatel Darjeeling tea; however, the neutral quality of the flan would take to any heavily aromatic tea like orange, vanilla, or lychee. The oranges work best with Yunnan, a black China tea with a distinct fruity aroma and aftertaste, but vanilla or a simple Ceylon black would be good choices, too.

To add an exotic switch to the garnish, instead of the Shredded Wheat, use 8 ounces/230 grams kataifi dough (available in Middle Eastern markets) or filo dough cut into thin julienne strips.

For the Flan

Melted butter or oil spray for ramekins

1 cup/240 milliliters milk 1 cup/240 milliliters heavy cream

3 tablespoons/42 grams Darjeeling muscatel tea leaves

Zest of 1 orange, removed from the orange in strips with a swivel-bladed vegetable peeler

2 whole cinnamon sticks

4 ounces/113 grams cream cheese

3/4 cup/150 grams granulated sugar

6 egg yolks

Preheat oven to 325°F/163°C. Brush the insides of six timbales with melted butter or oil spray. Set aside. (Ramekins or custard cups are great, or you can use a buttered 1-quart/1-liter casserole dish.)

In a 2-quart/2-liter heavy saucepan, heat the milk and cream with the tea leaves, orange zest, and cinnamon sticks only until the mixture comes to a simmer. Remove pan from heat and allow to infuse for 30 minutes. Sieve out solids and reserve the liquid.

In a large bowl, beat the cream cheese with the sugar until smooth, then stir in the egg yolks. Without aerating, blend in the tea-infused cream mixture. Sieve again, then pour into prepared timbales about 3/4 full. Prepare a water bath of boiling water deep enough in the pan to reach halfway up the sides of the molds. Carefully place the molds in the pan, and put the pan in the middle rack of the oven.

For the Oranges

2 large Shredded Wheat biscuits

4 tablespoons/2 ounces Yunnan tea leaves

3 cups/710 milliliters water

1 cup/200 grams granulated white sugar

2 teaspoons/10 grams cornstarch, dissolved in 1/4 cup/60 milliliters cold water

2 tablespoons unsalted (sweet) butter, melted

4 large navel oranges

Oil spray for pan

Bake for about 45 minutes, or until the flans feel firm and look lightly browned.

Note: If you are baking the flan in one larger dish, allow 10 to 15 minutes more baking time. Check for doneness. The center of the flan should be firm to the touch.

Remove from the oven and allow to cool at room temperature. The flan may be refrigerated at this point, or continue with the recipe and serve.

Carefully break the biscuits into long, separated strands and set aside.

Bring the tea leaves to a boil with 3 cups/710 milliliters of water. Sieve out leaves and return tea liquor to a clean saucepan. Add the sugar and thicken with the cornstarch dissolved in water. Cook over medium heat until the sauce clears and lightly coats a spoon. Set aside. (May be made a day in advance and then refrigerated at this point.)

Preheat oven to 350°F/177°C. Drizzle Shredded Wheat with melted butter and bake on a cookie sheet on the middle rack of the oven until golden brown, about 10 minutes. Set aside.

Preheat oven to broil. With a small, sharp paring knife, peel the oranges, removing the white pith and skin. Cut crosswise into 1/2-inch/ 1.5-centimeter rounds, removing any pits. Spray cookie sheet lightly with oil. Place the orange slices on the sheet and lightly brush them with some of the sauce. Broil about 3 inches/8 centimeters from the heating element until bubbly and hot. Remove from oven.

Mask each of 4 dessert plates with half the sauce. Arrange the broiled orange slices in an overlapping circle in the center of the plate.

Sprinkle the toasted Shredded Wheat over the orange slices, then carefully place the flan to the side. Drizzle both with the remaining sauce. Garnish with mint, as desired. Serve immediately. Four portions.

Chai Ice Cream

With its hint of fragrant spices, this ice cream works well as a foil for poached autumn fruit like a buttery pear or tart apple. Not overly sweet, it works equally well stuffed into a sweet-ripe summer peach or plum. When served with the merest bit of crisp, rich shortbread, it's an elegant finish to any spicy meal. The same procedure can be applied to any tea-based ice cream with a change in the complementary flavorings. Although we generally opt not to flavor tea, ice cream demands stronger flavors. Should you like a sweeter ice cream, add about 10 percent more sugar, honey, or some of each totaling 10 percent.

2 cups/500 milliliters heavy cream

1 cup/240 milliliters whole milk

4 slices fresh ginger root

1 tablespoon/4 grams whole allspice berries

1 tablespoon/3 grams whole cloves

12 whole green cardamom pods

3 whole cinnamon sticks, each about 3 inches long

1/2 cup/100 grams granulated white sugar

1/4 cup/60 milliliters honey

3 tablespoons/42 grams Chinese black tea such as Keemun

4 egg yolks

Large bowl of ice

Pinch of salt

1 teaspoon/5 milliliters real vanilla extract

In a large, heavy saucepan, bring the cream and milk to a boil with the spices, sugar, and honey. Add the tea and reduce mixture to a simmer. Remove from heat and infuse the tea for about 5 minutes. Sieve out solids and return liquid to saucepan.

In a small bowl, whisk the egg yolks and temper them by combining with a cup of the cream mixture. Add the whisked egg yolks to the saucepan and whisk together over medium heat until slightly thickened. Mixture should coat the back of a spoon. Using an instant-read thermometer, monitor the temperature of the mixture so it does not exceed 190°F/88°C. Do not overcook or the mixture will curdle.

Pour through a fine-meshed sieve into a bowl placed over a larger bowl of ice. Stir the mixture until cool and then place in refrigerator or freezer to chill further, about 15 minutes. Add salt and vanilla to blend.

Freeze using an old-fashioned ice cream maker filled with ice and salt, or freeze in a crank type ice cream machine using a canister that has been frozen as per the manufacturer's directions. Makes about 1 quart/1 liter; serves 6. This is exquisite alone but even more delicious over poached Bosc pears, as shown in the photo on page 92

Chai Ros Malai (Quick "Indian" Cream in Masala Chai)

Instead of using paneer, the fresh sweet cheese that is the basis for many Indian desserts, this recipe takes a shortcut by using ricotta cheese. Masala chai, augmented by some extra sweet spice, lends an intoxicating aroma to the sauce for this delectable cream.

1 pound/500 grams whole milk or part skim ricotta cheese

4 cups/1 liter milk

1/2 cup/100 grams granulated white sugar

5 whole green cardamom pods

1 stick cinnamon

4 whole cloves

2 tablespoons/30 milliliters Masala Chai concentrate

To remove any excess moisture, place the ricotta in a fine-meshed sieve set over a bowl. Refrigerate overnight if time allows, covered. Draining the cheese for only a few hours in the refrigerator will do in a pinch.

Make creamy sauce by bringing the milk, sugar, spices, and Masala Chai to a boil in a saucepan. Cook, stirring frequently and deeply into the bottom of the pot until the mixture reduces enough to coat the back of a wooden spoon. Remove from the pot, pour through a fine-meshed sieve to remove solids, and place the sauce in a bowl. Cool and then refrigerate, covered, until it is thoroughly chilled.

Remove refrigerated ricotta cheese and sauce from the refrigerator. Pour a small amount of the sauce on each place. Using 2 large soup spoons dipped in hot water, form the ricotta into oval shaped portions. Center 1 ricotta oval on each plate and mask thoroughly with the remaining sauce. Serves 6.

Chai Scones

Although we intentionally omitted representative dishes from the traditional English afternoon tea table, the following is our exception, offering it merely as a foil for Darjeeling Peach Conserve (see recipe, page 42; see photo, page 43).

The rich, warm spiciness of Masala Chai, a peppery spicy tea so typical in Northern India, is fast becoming the cappuccino of teas in America. This time,

Masala Chai finds its way into these buttery scones. The dough can be made in advance if well wrapped and frozen at 0°F/-18°C for about a month.

The recipe uses a premade Masala Chai concentrate now readily available in supermarkets. (See sources at back of the book.) The spices have been enhanced, and a mixture of cinnamon and sugar is sprinkled on top of the scones just before baking. For a lower-fat version, make these with milk instead of cream or half-and-half.

1 pound or 3³/₄ cups/500 grams all-purpose flour, lightly packed

¹/₂ cup/100 grams firmly packed brown sugar

1 teaspoon/2 grams baking powder

1 teaspoon/2 grams ground cinnamon

1 teaspoon/2 grams ground cardamom

1 teaspoon/2 grams ground ginger

4 ounces/115 grams unsalted (sweet) butter

2 egg yolks

6 ounces/180 milliliters heavy cream or half-and-half

5 ounces/150 milliliters Masala Chai concentrate

Egg wash made from 2 egg yolks mixed with 2 tablespoons/30 milliliters heavy cream or milk

1 cup/200 grams granulated white sugar mixed with one teaspoon/ 2 grams ground cinnamon, for topping

Sift all dry ingredients together and place into a bowl of an electric mixer. Add butter. Mix on low speed until the mixture resembles coarse meal. In a small bowl, combine egg yolks, heavy cream or half-and-half, and Masala Chai concentrate. Add the wet mixture to the dry ingredients and mix just until combined; do not overmix.

Preheat oven to 425°F/218°C. Remove mixture from bowl to a lightly floured surface and knead briefly. Divide into 2 equal parts and flatten each into a round measuring about 7 inches/18 centimeters in diameter by ¹/₂ inch/2 centimeters thick. With a knife dipped in flour, score each round into 8 equal wedges. Brush with the egg wash and prick decoratively with a fork, if desired. Sprinkle with cinnamon sugar mixture and place in oven for 15 minutes, or until golden brown. Let cool slightly on a rack and cut into 8 wedges each.

Serve with the Darjeeling Peach Conserve (see recipe, page 42), Devonshire cream, or softly whipped sweetened cream. The recipe makes 16 hefty pieces, but it can easily be halved or doubled as desired.

Chocolate Melting Moments Torte with Tea Crème Anglaise

This is a rich yet light dessert that's easily made in advance. This elegant torte incorporates brewed tea in its batter, which intensifies the deep chocolate flavor.

8 ounces/230 grams bittersweet chocolate (using good quality pays off with an exquisite rich taste), cut into small pieces for ease of melting

4 ounces/115 grams unsalted (sweet) butter

2 tablespoons/28 grams Indian black tea, such as Tippy Assam

1/2 cup/120 milliliters water

1 ounce/28 grams unsweetened cocoa powder

5 eggs, separated

1/2 cup/100 grams granulated white sugar

1 teaspoon/5 milliliters pure vanilla extract

1/2 cup/100 grams flour

2 tablespoons/28 grams malted milk powder

Butter and flour for coating the cake pan

Confectioner's sugar for topping the finished cake

Preheat oven to 350°F/177°C.

Melt the chocolate and butter together in a heatproof bowl set over simmering water. Brew the tea in 1/2 cup/120 milliliters of boiling water, steeping for 3 minutes. Sieve out the leaves. Dissolve the cocoa in the brewed tea and stir until smooth. Blend the cocoa-tea mixture into the chocolate and butter mixture.

Separate the eggs. Stir egg yolks into above chocolate mixture and set aside.

Place the whites in a perfectly fat-free bowl of an electric mixer and beat with whisk attachment until foamy. Add the sugar in a slow, steady stream and continue beating until billowy peaks are achieved. Fold in vanilla to blend. Do not overbeat or the whites will be dry, grainy, and difficult to fold into the chocolate mixture.

In a small bowl, mix flour and malted milk powder together. Then, fold egg whites alternately with the flour and malted milk powder into the chocolate mixture just until blended. Do not overmix, as the batter should remain light and airy.

Pour the batter into a lightly greased and floured 8-inch/20-centimeter springform pan. Bake for approximately 40 minutes. Do not overbake (a toothpick or skewer inserted into the center of the cake will have some fudgy batter clinging to it). The cake will rise in the oven and fall somewhat after being cooled.

Tea Crème Anglaise

1 cup/250 milliliters whole milk

2 tablespoons/28 grams Indian black tea leaves, such as Assam or English breakfast blend

3 egg yolks

Bowl of ice

¹/₂ cup/100 grams granulated sugar

Tea Crème Anglaise

In a heavy 2-quart/2-liter saucepan, bring the milk and tea leaves to a boil. Turn off the heat and steep the tea for 10 minutes. Sieve out leaves and reserve the tea-infused milk.

In a medium-size bowl, whisk the egg yolks and sugar together until the sugar is dissolved and the mixture is light yellow.

Reheat the tea-milk mixture until hot and blend in ¹/₂ cup/120 milliliters of it to temper the egg and sugar mixture, then add the entire egg and sugar mixture to the remaining milk. Whisk constantly in a saucepan over medium heat until a spoon is lightly coated (the temperature on an instant-read thermometer should read about 190°F/88°C, and a fingertip dragged across the mixture should leave a mark on the surface of the sauce). Do not overcook or the mixture will curdle.

Pour immediately through a fine-meshed sieve into a bowl set over ice. Stir to cool quickly. Chill in refrigerator until ready to serve.

Presentation: Sprinkle confectioner's sugar through a fine-meshed sieve over the top of the cake. Sauce each plate with a small amount of the chilled Tea Crème Anglaise and place a wedge of cake on top of the sauce. Serve immediately. Yields 6 portions.

Earl Grey Truffles

These rich truffles are mellowed with the clean, sweet taste of candied orange peel in the chocolate plus the bergamot scent to the Darjeeling tea that infuses the cream. As always, the finest ingredients are critical to the success of this recipe, and we suggest high-quality bittersweet chocolate, like French Valrhona or Cluizel, Venezuelan El Rey, or Spanish Chocovic. Dusting each creamy square of truffle with pure, bittersweet cocoa powder provides an exquisite counterbalance to the sweetness of the truffle.

Strips of candied peel from one orange, homemade (see procedure below) or store-bought

$\frac{1}{2}$ cup/100 grams granulated sugar

16 ounces/475 milliliters heavy cream

2 tablespoons/28 grams Earl Grey Imperial tea leaves

21 ounces/600 grams finely chopped bittersweet chocolate

Bittersweet cocoa powder for dusting the truffles

Make candied peels by cutting strips from one brightly colored orange, making sure no white inner pith is used, as the pith will make it bitter. Boil the peel in water for 5 minutes and drain. Boil again in fresh water and drain. Make a simple syrup by boiling 1 cup/240 milliliters of water with $\frac{1}{2}$ cup/100 grams granulated sugar until clear. Cook the peel for the third time in the simple syrup for about 5 minutes. Remove peel from syrup and allow to drain on a wire rack. Set aside.

In a heavy 2-quart/2-liter saucepan, bring the cream and the tea to a boil. Remove from heat, allow to infuse for about 15 minutes, and then strain through a fine-meshed sieve into a bowl. Add the chocolate and stir lightly with a wooden spoon until the chocolate is melted and the mixture is perfectly smooth. To retain its characteristic dense, fudgy texture, do not aerate the chocolate mixture.

Purée the candied orange peel in a food processor along with approximately 1 cup/240 milliliters of the chocolate mixture.

Line an 8x10-inch/20x25-centimeter baking sheet with parchment. Pour half of the remaining chocolate mixture into the pan. Pour all of the orange peel and chocolate mixture over the chocolate in the pan and spread evenly with a spatula. Pour the remaining chocolate mixture over this layer. Smooth the top with a spatula and cover tightly with baking parchment. Chill until firm, about 2 hours.

With a heavy knife, cut the chilled chocolate into 72 equal squares. Place on a parchment-lined sheet pan and sift the cocoa powder over the truffles, coating light and evenly. Place in small candy cups if desired and arrange on a platter and refrigerate until 10 minutes before serving. These are best served cold, but not rock solid, as their flavor opens up after a few minutes at room temperature. This recipe makes 72 bite-sized but rich truffles; how many make a serving is up to you!

Note: These may be made a day in advance and kept refrigerated until serving.

Fresh Peach-Darjeeling Sorbet

Teas from the Darjeeling district of Northern India are prized for their delicate flavor and aroma. Tasting one particular variety in that region from a single estate called Orange Valley, with its beautifully flowery, fruity character, we were reminded of peaches. Thus, a sorbet was born.

When you're looking for a light but satisfying ending to a spicy or well-sauced meal, try this sorbet. With a hint of brewed fine tea providing a background note, this refreshing dessert captures the round ripeness of summer peaches in every frozen bite. Pouring chilled tea over the sorbet before serving adds flavor and just the right bit of frosty crunch for added texture.

Note: Don't resort to out-of-season fruit, which simply cannot compare with the highly perfumed fruits of summer available at your local farmer's market or roadside stand. Although this recipe may be made using canned peach nectar in place of the fresh peach, reduce the sugar accordingly. For pure peach flavor, it's worth waiting until the season's right.

During that brief moment in late spring or early summer when apricots are at their peak, feel free to substitute them for the peaches and garnish each serving with fresh slices of that fruit if desired.

1 cup/240 milliliters water

2 cups/400 grams granulated white sugar

4 tablespoons/56 grams Darjeeling tea leaves

2 cups/475 milliliters puréed, peeled, and pitted ripe peaches

Juice of l lemon

Garnishes: 2 cups/475 milliliters fresh peaches, peeled and thinly sliced; mint sprigs

Place 4 freezer-safe goblets into the freezer.

Brew 1 tablespoon/14 grams Darjeeling tea leaves in 1 cup/240 milliliters hot (180°F/82°C) water and infuse for about 2 minutes. Sieve out tea the tea leaves and reserve the liquid. Cool and chill, covered, in refrigerator until serving time.

Heat the water and sugar to boil. Let cool for 5 minutes. Add 4 tablespoons/56 grams tea leaves and infuse for 2 minutes. Sieve to remove the tea leaves. (Save the leaves for a second infusion and drink up!) Add the peach purée and lemon juice and freeze until firm using any of the following methods: For the creamiest product, pour into a

For Sauce

1 tablespoon/14 grams Darjeeling tea leaves and 1 cup/240 milliliters water, for presentation

tabletop, self-contained, no-ice-needed ice cream machine; for a somewhat more granular textured ice, freeze the mixture in a canister-type electric ice cream maker that uses rock salt and ice cubes to freeze the mixture; or freeze in a stainless steel bowl until firm, about 8 hours. Process in batches in a food processor or blender just until slushy and somewhat creamy and serve immediately.

Yields approximately 1 quart/1 liter. Place 1 large scoop into each chilled, frosted goblet. Pour about $1/4$ cup/60 milliliters of the chilled brewed tea over each serving and garnish with sliced peaches and a sprig of fresh mint, if desired. Serves 4 to 6.

Green Tea–Poached Asian Pears with Pistachio Cream Sauce

This refreshing dessert, a year-round treat, is edged with a rumor of mint for a touch of luxury. Its complex taste belies its simple method of preparation. Look for fruit that is unbruised with a taut skin.

4 unblemished Asian pears

1 cup/200 grams granulated white sugar

2 cups/475 milliliters freshly brewed green tea, such as Dragonwell, using water at 180 to 185°F/82 to 85°C

1 2-inch/5-centimeter piece of fresh ginger root, peeled and sliced into thin coins

Peel of half an average-sized lemon

1 large sprig of fresh mint

Garnish: fresh mint leaves, if desired

Pistachio Cream Sauce

1 cup/240 milliliters nonfat plain yogurt, well drained

1/2 cup/120 milliliters buttermilk

1 teaspoon/5 milliliters pure maple syrup

1 cup/130 grams shelled, skinned, coarsely chopped natural pistachio nuts

Chill 4 goblets. Peel the pears and core with a corer or a small paring knife, being sure to remove the tart center area of each. Place the sugar, green tea, ginger root, lemon peel, and mint in a medium-size saucepan large enough to hold the 4 pears in a single layer.

Over medium heat, bring the mixture to just under a boil, or until the sugar is fully dissolved. Reduce the heat to a simmer and add the peeled and cored pears. Cook for about 15 to 20 minutes. The pears will remain firm. Cool to room temperature and then refrigerate, covered. Meanwhile, make the Pistachio Cream Sauce.

Pistachio Cream Sauce

In a small bowl, whisk together the yogurt, buttermilk, and maple syrup. Add the nuts and store mixture in refrigerator until your guests are ready to eat.

Assembly: Remove pears from poaching liquid, drain well, and place 1 each in 4 chilled goblets. Mask with the sauce and serve immediately, garnished with fresh mint leaves if desired. Serves 4.

Grilled Pineapple with Vanilla Tea Crème Anglaise

The sweetness of pineapple is greatly enhanced by the creamy vanilla sauce with just a hint of maple syrup to bridge all the flavors. This is a dessert that simply explodes in the mouth.

Vanilla Tea Crème Anglaise

1 cup/240 milliliters 2 percent milk

1 cup/240 milliliters heavy cream

1 cup/200 grams granulated sugar

1 ounce/28 grams aromatic tea leaves, such as vanilla

4 large eggs

Large bowl of ice

1 tablespoon/15 milliliters dark rum

For the Pineapple

1 whole large pineapple, ripe but not overripe, depending on size

Unflavored oil spray, such as canola

1/2 cup/120 milliliters pure maple syrup

Bring the milk and cream to a boil, then add the sugar and tea leaves. Remove from heat and infuse for 30 minutes. Sieve out the solids through a fine-meshed sieve and return liquid to a clean saucepan. Reheat until hot and then remove 1/2 cup/120 milliliters of that liquid to a bowl. In the bowl, temper the eggs with the liquid, whisking until well blended. Add the tempered eggs back to the rest of the liquid in the saucepan and cook over medium heat, whisking constantly until the sauce reaches 185 to 190°F/85 to 88°C. It should coat the back of a spoon. Place a heatproof bowl over an ice bath; pour the mixture through a fine-meshed sieve into the bowl to cool it quickly. Add the rum and put the mixture into a covered bowl and refrigerate until ready to serve.

With a serrated knife, remove the ends of the pineapple, then, following the contour of the fruit, remove the shell. Cut lengthwise in quarters, then remove the pithy core. Slice across into 1/2-inch/ 1-centimeter slices.

To prepare the pineapple, line a cookie sheet with foil that has been sprayed with the oil. Lay the pineapple slices on the foil. Place sheet on a rack in the broiler at least 4 inches/10 centimeters from the heating element. Broil for about 2 minutes and then invert the tray onto a second cookie sheet, lined with foil and lightly sprayed with the oil. Broil for 2 more minutes. When cooked, drizzle with maple syrup.

Assembly: Fan out slices on a platter and serve with a ramekin of the sauce. Serves 6.

Honeydew Green Tea Frappe

Green tea is especially clean tasting, grassy, and refreshing served iced. Here the intoxicating perfume of a hauntingly sweet honeydew melon is perfectly layered with the crisp spring taste of green tea, either Chinese Dragonwell (Lung Ching), Japanese Sencha, or even a green Darjeeling tea from India. This frothy drink, the pale color of Chinese celadon porcelain, cools you even during the most sweltering hot spell.

3 tablespoons/42 grams loosely packed green tea leaves of your choice

2 ounces/60 grams crystallized ginger, roughly chopped

4 cups/1 liter cubed ripe honeydew melon

2 cups/500 milliliters ice cubes made from distilled water

Superfine sugar to taste

Garnishes: Thinly sliced honeydew melon, crystallized ginger in long pieces, and fresh ginger juice.

Chill 4 tall glasses. Brew the tea leaves in 1 quart/1 liter of 185°F/85°C water, allowing them to steep 4 minutes. Pour the tea through a fine-meshed sieve, pressing hard on the leaves to extract all the liquid. Add the crystallized ginger to the brewed tea and let cool until it becomes infused with the ginger flavor, about 15 minutes, or longer if time allows. Chill in refrigerator until cold. Pass liquid through sieve to remove ginger pieces. (The ginger pieces can be saved to add to a chicken salad or fruit compote, as desired. For a more spicy flavor, fresh ginger root can be substituted.)

Purée the melon and ice in the jar of an electric blender. Add tea-ginger infusion and process just to blend. Pour into tall chilled glasses and sweeten to taste with superfine sugar. Add a dash of fresh ginger juice if available. Garnish with a thin slice of honeydew wrapped with a slice of crystallized ginger. Yields 4 12-ounce/350-gram servings.

Milk Chocolate Torte with Assam Tea Ganache

This is a rich, special-occasion dessert that uses dark milk chocolate, an interesting category of chocolate that has about 41 percent cocoa content versus the nearly 70 percent of a pure dark chocolate. This provides a taste with the bite of dark chocolate but the additional sweetness of milk, and often more sugar. It makes this ganache, well, divine. See Appendix D: Resources for Unusual Ingredients for chocolate sources, although most gourmet food shops carry them.

8 ounces/240 grams dark milk chocolate (41% cocoa content)

4 tablespoons/56 grams Tippy Assam tea leaves (or an Assam of your choice)

1/2 cup/120 milliliters water

4 ounces/120 grams sweet butter

4 large eggs, separated

1/3 cup/40 grams all-purpose flour, sifted twice

2 teaspoons/10 grams malted milk powder

Preheat oven to 350°F/177°C. Lightly coat the bottom and sides of an 8-inch/20-centimeter springform or regular cake pan with non-flavored aeroslized spray. Line the bottom with a circle of parchment paper.

In a double boiler or a stainless steel bowl set over a pan of simmering water, melt the chocolate. In a separate small saucepan, bring the tea leaves, water, and butter to a boil. Remove from heat and stir to melt the butter, allowing the tea leaves to infuse in the water-butter mixture for about 3 minutes. Pass through a fine sieve into the chocolate. Stir to blend. Allow to cool for about 15 minutes.

Separate the eggs, placing the whites into a perfectly clean, fat-free bowl of an electric mixer and the yolks into the chocolate mixture. Beat whites until soft peaks form. Sift flour and malted milk powder together and then fold in egg whites. Fold this flour-malted milk powder mixture gently but thoroughly into the chocolate base. Pour into a prepared cake pan and bake for about 35 minutes, or until the cake appears firm, but not dry. This cake is very moist inside and will fall as it cools. Make the ganache.

Assam Ganache

7 ounces/210 milliliters heavy cream

*2 tablespoons/28 grams Tippy Assam
    tea leaves*

*7 ounces/200 grams dark milk
    chocolate, cut into $1/_2$-inch/
    1-centimeter pieces*

*1 tablespoon/15 grams unsalted
    (sweet) butter*

In a heavy 1-quart/1-liter saucepan, bring the cream and tea leaves to a boil. Remove from heat and allow to infuse further for 3 minutes. Pass through a fine-meshed sieve into a bowl set over a pot of simmering water. Slowly add the chocolate and gently stir to blend, without aerating. Add the butter and stir until completely melted. Set aside.

Assembly: Line a cookie sheet with parchment paper or foil. Place the cake on a cooling rack, then place the rack on the cookie sheet. Pour the ganache over the cake, using a spatula to spread the ganache evenly as needed. Allow to set. Scrape up any ganache that drips off the cake and pour to cover the cake a second time. (Reheat slightly over a pot of simmering water, if necessary, to loosen the mixture.) Cool at room temperature. Makes 1 torte that serves 6 to 8.

Note: If your kitchen is hot, place the cake in the refrigerator just until the ganache sets and feels dry to the touch. Remove the cake from the refrigerator about 20 minutes prior to serving and allow it to adjust to room temperature.

Jasmine-Lemongrass Tea Sorbet

This sorbet is an ideal example of an intermission, the delicate and refreshing pause between courses. With its flowery roundness of flavor, Chinese Jasmine tea is an ideal candidate to star in a frozen ice. Its heady fragrance is made more intoxicating with the addition of lemongrass (Cymbopogon citratus or citronella), much favored in Southeast Asian cooking. As a dessert, this tops off any meal with palate-cleansing freshness.

1 quart/1 liter water

2 cups/400 grams granulated white sugar

12 stalks lemongrass, using only the bottom 6 inches of each, thinly sliced to expose as much surface as possible for the most intense infusion

4 tablespoons/56 grams Jasmine Yin Hao tea leaves

Juice of one large lemon

Garnishes: Drained, chilled lychee or rambutan, available in cans at Asian markets, plus some mint leaves.

Chill the goblets until frosted. Bring the water and sugar to boil and add the lemongrass. Infuse for about 15 minutes. Add the Jasmine tea and infuse for 5 more minutes. Pour the liquid through a fine-meshed sieve and let cool. Add the lemon juice and chill in the refrigerator. When cold, place in the freezer until quite firm. Any one of the following methods are suitable: For the creamiest product, pour into a tabletop, self-contained, no-ice-needed ice cream machine. For a more granular textured ice, freeze the mixture in a canister-type electric ice cream maker that uses rock salt and ice cubes to chill. Or, freeze in your freezer in a stainless steel bowl until firm, about 8 hours. Process in batches in a food processor or blender until slushy and somewhat creamy.

Remove goblets from freezer and fill with sorbet. Garnish each with tropical fruit and mint leaves as desired. Makes about 1 quart/1 liter, enough for 6.

Peaches in Kenya Tea Sauce

The fragrance of these ripe, white-fleshed peaches in summer is only matched by the fragrance of the Kenya tea in which they are poached. This dessert, an example of utter simplicity, takes just a bit of sugar to mellow the sauce and some care in peeling the fruit without bruising. Serve plain, either warm or cold, or add a shower of fresh berries and a dollop of yogurt or whipped cream for an even prettier presentation.

2 tablespoons/28 grams Kenya black tea leaves

2 cups/500 milliliters water

¹/₂ cup/100 grams sugar

4 ripe white-fleshed peaches, peeled, halved, and pitted (yellow-fleshed peaches are fine if the white-fleshed variety are unavailable.)

Optional accompaniments: Fresh berries in season, yogurt, or whipped cream, lightly sweetened

Bring the tea and water to a boil. Steep 1 minute and pass the brewed tea through a sieve. Discard the tea leaves.

Add sugar to the tea liquor and heat over medium heat just to dissolve the sugar, about 1 minute. Gently add the peaches and cook them until tender but not mushy, about 5 minutes. Remove peaches to a heatproof bowl and reserve.

Continue to heat the poaching liquid over high heat, about 10 minutes, or until it is reduced by half and can coat a spoon lightly.

Pour the reduced liquid over the peaches and cool at room temperature. They can be served warm, or to serve chilled, cover and refrigerate until dessert time.

As desired, add berries, yogurt, or whipped cream. Yields 4 servings.

Real Green Tea Ice Cream with Sesame-Caramel Sauce

Good-quality Japanese Sencha green tea is best, but any tea, whether finely powdered or whole leaf, will lend the distinctive flavor imprint of green tea to this refreshing combination of cool and cream. The nutty, toasty personality of green tea is the ideal match for the rich Sesame-Caramel Sauce.

Note: This version has only the faintest tinge of green, so don't expect a screaming green color, unless, that is, you wish to add it.

2 cups/500 milliliters whole milk

¹/₄ cup/50 grams green tea leaves

2 cups/500 milliliters heavy cream

³/₄ cup/150 grams granulated sugar

Finely grated zest of 1 lime (reserve lime for the sauce)

Few drops of pure vanilla extract

Sesame-Caramel Sauce

2 tablespoons/12 grams sesame seeds

1 cup/200 grams granulated sugar

1 cup/240 milliliters water

Juice of 1 lime (reserved from the Real Green Tea Ice Cream recipe)

¹/₂ cup/120 milliliters heavy cream

Warm water, as needed, to thin sauce

In a heavy saucepan, bring the milk and tea to a boil. Remove from heat and infuse for 1 minute. Pour through a fine-meshed sieve into a heatproof bowl, pressing hard on the tea leaves to extract as much of the liquid as possible. Return to a clean saucepan. Add the cream, sugar, and lime zest. Bring to a boil and stir until sugar dissolves completely. Cool, then add the vanilla extract. Chill until cold, then freeze using the machine of your choice, following the manufacturer's directions. While the ice cream is freezing, prepare the sauce.

Sesame-Caramel Sauce

Toast sesame seeds until golden, then set aside. In a heavy 1-quart/ 1-liter saucepan, bring sugar, water, and lime juice to a boil over medium to high heat. Cook until golden brown, swirling the pan a few times, but do not stir. Do not allow to burn. Meanwhile, in a small saucepan, heat the cream until warm, then add warmed cream, a few tablespoons/milliliters at a time, to the sugar mixture. Stir gently with a wooden spoon to blend, being careful not to get splattered, as this mixture foams up the sides of the pan. When blended, add the toasted sesame seeds to the sugar and cream mixture. Because this sesame-caramel sauce will thicken upon standing, thin as needed with warm water prior to serving.

If the sauce is made ahead and refrigerated, reheat gently just until liquid, then cool to room temperature before pouring over the servings of ice cream.

Assembly: Dish out scoops of ice cream into chilled bowls, then pour sauce over each portion. Makes approximately 1 quart/1 liter of ice cream for 4 to 6 servings. Serve additional sauce on the side.

Snowy Silver Needle Sorbet

This light dessert is unsurpassed for refreshment when the heat of summer rolls around. A study in white, this frozen treat, surmounted with some well-chilled canned Asian rambutan or lychee fruit (which are also white), would end a spicy Asian meal on a satisfying note. Serve it in the darkest colored bowls or goblets you have to set off its pristine whiteness beautifully. White tea weighs almost nothing, so be generous when measuring to infuse the syrup for this iced treat.

1 cup/200 grams sugar and 1 cup/ 250 milliliters water to make a yield of 1 ³/₄ cups/420 milliliters simple syrup

2 heaping tablespoons/30 grams white tea leaves (Silver Needle or Yintzen, for example) steeped in 1 cup/250 milliliters of water

Juice of 1 lime (about 1 tablespoon/ 15 milliliters)

1 can (approximately 12 ounces/240 grams) lychee or rambutan, well drained and chilled

Prepare the simple syrup by bringing 1 cup/200 grams of sugar and 1 cup/250 milliliters of water to a boil. Cook just until the sugar dissolves thoroughly. Allow to cool. Steep tea leaves in 170°F/77°C water for about 5 minutes. Pass through a fine-meshed sieve placed over a heatproof bowl, pressing hard on the tea leaves to extract as much of the infused liquid as possible.

When room temperature, combine brewed tea with sugar syrup. Stir in the lime juice. Chill, covered, until cold and freeze in an ice cream machine according to the manufacturer's instructions. This dessert may also be made by freezing the mixture in a stainless steel bowl, stirring occasionally to break up as many of the ice crystals that form as possible. When firm, serve in iced bowls or goblets, garnished with lychee, rambutan, Asian pear apples, thinly sliced, or other Asian fruit. Serves 4 to 6.

White Chocolate Mousse with Bitter Lime Sauce

The floral notes in a Jasmine-scented green tea insinuate themselves beauti-
fully into the white chocolate. Good quality white chocolate provides the best
results in this yin-yang ensemble. The bitter lime sauce sets off the sweetness
of the white chocolate with mouth-satisfying results.

The Mousse

8 ounces/240 grams fine quality
*   white chocolate, finely chopped*

1/2 ounce/14 grams loose-leaf
*   Jasmine tea leaves*

4 ounces/120 milliliters heavy
*   cream to infuse the tea leaves*

4 ounces/120 milliliters heavy
*   cream, whippped*

Bitter Lime Sauce

1 cup/240 milliliters fresh lime juice

1 cup/200 grams granulated sugar

1 tablespoon/14 grams cornstarch
*   mixed with 2 tablespoons/*
*   30 milliliters cold water*

1 teaspoon/5 grams unsalted (sweet)
*   butter, softened*

Zest of 1 lime, finely grated

Prepare the bitter lime sauce first as follows then set aside. Bring the lime juice and sugar to a boil, then cook over medium heat until sugar is dissolved. In a small bowl, dissolve the cornstarch in water then add to the lime juice mixture. Stir until the mixture thickens slightly. Allow to cool. Add butter and grated lime zest and stir to combine.

To prepare the mousse, chop the white chocolate and place in a heatproof stainless steel bowl. Set aside. In a heavy 1-quart/1-liter saucepan, bring the cream and tea leaves infusion to a boil, then remove from heat. Infuse for 1 hour at room temperature. Over a bowl, pass the mixture through a fine-meshed sieve, pressing hard on the tea leaves to extract as much of the tea-infused cream as possible. Bring this liquid to a boil again and then pour over the white chocolate in the bowl. Stir until chocolate is completely melted and the mixture is smooth. Set aside at room temperature to cool. Do not allow this mixture to set.

In an electric mixer or using a whisk, whip the remaining cream to soft peaks and fold into the cooled white chocolate mixture. Pour into individual serving ramekins or into a small loaf pan lined with parchment or plastic wrap. Chill until cold. If using a loaf pan, unmold onto a serving platter, slice into 1/2-inch/1-centimeter slices and serve the sauce on the side. Serves 6.

Tea Beverages

Tea invites your creativity like no other drink. It makes a wonderful base with fresh fruit, sorbets, and fruit syrups as iced drinks; or mixed with milk and spices, your favorite whiskey for a toddy, or fruit syrups as hot drinks. Nothing soothes like a hot cup in winter, nothing refreshes quite like an icy glass of tea in summer—yet that is only the beginning. Here are a few of our favorites to inspire you.

Chocolate Chai

Iced Tea with Lemongrass Syrup

Iced Tea Lemonade with Lemon-Rosemary Sorbet

Keemun-Kantaloupe Kooler

Chocolate Chai

There must be as many chai recipes as there are Indians, each chai flavored with a slightly different combination or proportion of spices. This icy granita-in-a-glass uses Cameroon tea (finely ground black tea with a hint of chocolate) and some bittersweet chocolate, along with the traditional cardamom, cinnamon, and allspice. Here is a chai that was born to be served iced.

Unlike most recipes for chai, which use whole milk, nonfat milk works well here. The chocolate adds a depth of flavor to this rich-tasting, elegant dessert. Make the mixture in advance to keep you free when guests arrive.

1 quart/1 liter milk (nonfat, lowfat, or full fat, as desired)

$1/_2$ cup/100 grams granulated sugar

2 ounces/60 grams bittersweet chocolate, finely chopped

2 tablespoons/28 grams Cameroon (Chinese or Indian black will also work)

6 cardamom pods, crushed

2 whole cinnamon sticks

4 allspice berries, crushed

1 vanilla bean, slit lengthwise to reveal its seeds (or 1 teaspoon/ 5 milliliters pure vanilla extract)

Garnish: four cinnamon sticks

In a 2-quart/2-liter saucepan, place all of the ingredients except the garnish. Bring to a simmer, then whisk the mixture lightly to make sure that the chocolate is fully dissolved. Cook over low heat for about 5 minutes. Remove from the heat and infuse for 10 minutes. When cool, sieve out solids. Chill the mixture until cold and then freeze in a shallow pan or baking dish.

Place 4 tall glasses (about 12-ounce/350-milliliter capacity) in the freezer about 1 hour before serving. Just before serving, break up the frozen mixture into rough chunks and whirl in the blender until slushy. Pour into the chilled glasses and garnish each with a cinnamon stick.

Note: If using a vanilla bean, wash and dry it after use. Place it in a container of granulated sugar to give a lovely fragrance to the sugar.

Iced Tea with Lemongrass Syrup

Here, two powerful Asian flavors meet in a glass. Perfect when the weather heats up, this simple drink shows off the flowery quality of the best Jasmine tea from China. In the southeastern part of China, green tea leaves are layered at night with Jasmine flowers plucked that morning. The Chinese Jasmine flower only blossoms at night, so this is the perfect time to infuse tea with the fragrance of this very special flower. The subtle tang of lemongrass adds the right edge of tartness.

Lemongrass Syrup

2 cups/450 grams granulated white sugar

2 cups/500 milliliters water

6 fat stalks fresh lemongrass, coarsely chopped and mashed

note

The above quantities are intentionally generous to allow for leftovers since the syrup may be used to flavor seasonal fruit salads or to perk up fruits that look better than they taste. This syrup keeps at least a month in the refrigerator and may also be used to flavor dressings or to drizzle over fresh fruit such as starfruit, melon, pineapple, mango, and papaya.

The Tea

2 tablespoons/28 grams Jasmine tea leaves

1 quart/1 liter cold water

Garnishes: 1 lemongrass stalk, $^1/_4$ of a fresh pineapple, cored, thinly sliced into triangular wedges

Make the syrup by bringing the sugar and water to boil. When boiling, add the lemongrass stalks, which have been coarsely chopped and mashed with a mallet or rolling pin to release their flavor. Remove from the heat and let stand until cool. Strain through a fine-meshed sieve, extracting as much liquid as possible. Pour into a glass jar, cover, and refrigerate.

Brew the tea by heating water to 180 to 185°F/82 to 85°C. Infuse for 3 minutes. Strain and reserve.

Pour about 1 tablespoon/15 milliliters of the lemongrass syrup into each tall glass. Top with tea, add ice as desired. Garnish with a stick of lemongrass inserted into a thin wedge of fresh pineapple. Serves 2.

Iced Tea Lemonade with Lemon-Rosemary Sorbet

The delicate, aromatic black Darjeeling gains a new dimension with a scoop of puckery citrus-herbal sorbet. Using tea for the ice cubes ensures that you won't dilute the flavor of the brewed tea. For a more assertive tea flavor, use Assam.

1 cup/240 grams sugar

1 cup/250 milliliters water

4 sprigs fresh rosemary

Juice from 2 to 3 lemons, about $^1/_2$ to $^3/_4$ cup/120 to 175 milliliters

Zest of 2 lemons, grated

2 tablespoons/28 grams lightly packed Darjeeling tea leaves

1 quart/1 liter spring water

Superfine sugar to sweeten tea to taste

Garnish: 4 sprigs of fresh rosemary

Bring the sugar and 1 cup/250 milliliters of water to boil and cook until sugar clears. Remove rosemary sprigs from the stems by rubbing your fingers from the top of the stalk downward toward the root end. Discard stems. Add rosemary sprigs to the sugar syrup and simmer over low heat for about 5 minutes, then cool. Refrigerate covered in an airtight container.

Combine the syrup with the lemon juice and lemon zest. Freeze in an ice cream freezer according to the manufacturer's directions.

Bring 1 quart/1 liter of water to just under a boil, about 190°F/88°C. Add the tea leaves and brew for 3 minutes. Pass tea through a fine-meshed sieve, extracting as much liquid as possible, then discard the leaves. Cool, then sweeten to taste. Pour half the brewed tea into an ice cube tray and freeze. Chill remaining tea. To serve, pour chilled tea into tall glasses, add tea ice cubes, and top with a scoop of the Lemon-Rosemary Sorbet. Garnish with a sprig of fresh rosemary as desired. Makes approximately 4 8-ounce/250-milliliter servings of tea lemonade, each topped with $^1/_4$ of the sorbet.

Keemun-Kantaloupe Kooler

*A highly perfumed cantaloupe in season is a deliciously sweet backdrop for
the pronounced tea flavor of this summer drink. Whenever the temperature gets
uncomfortably hot, you'll be "kool" with this refreshing tea-based beverage.*

*1 large ripe cantaloupe, peeled and
seeded, about 2 pounds/1 kilogram*

*Superfine sugar for coating the rims of
the glasses and to taste*

*2 tablespoons/28 grams Keemun (or
any other black tea) leaves*

2 cups/500 milliliters water

Juice of 2 limes

*12 ice cubes, about 1 ounce/
30 grams each*

*Garnishes: Wedges of cantaloupe;
wedges of lime; sprigs of mint
leaves, stems intact.*

Cut 4 thin crescent wedges of cantaloupe as garnish and reserve in the freezer.

Dip 4 tall glasses in water, then dip the rims into sugar to coat. Freeze glasses.

Cut the remaining melon into 1-inch/2.5-centimeter chunks.

Brew 2 tablespoons/28 grams of Keemun leaves in 2 cups/500 milliliters of water at 180°F/82°C. Steep about 3 minutes, then sieve out the tea leaves and reserve the liquid. Chill until cold.

Just before serving, place the melon, chilled tea, and lime juice into a blender jar. Add ice cubes gradually, puréeing mixture until smooth and frothy. Taste and add sugar as desired. Purée again.

Remove the glasses from the freezer.

Garnishes: Pour kooler into the frozen glasses and top each with a melon crescent, a wedge of lime, and a sprig of mint. Serve immediately. Yields 4 servings.

Appendices

Pairing Teas with Food

Although one can certainly have a meal of tea-infused foods, each using differ-ent teas, it is best to pair a dish with a beverage made of the same tea. For example, Jade Shrimp in Lung Ching Tea (page 46) tastes wonderful with a Dragonwell (Lung Ching), but you may discover other greens that work as well.

As always, our choices for teas are suggestions. It's easiest to choose a tea that either matches or is similar to the one used in the preparation of a dish. But, surprisingly, light-tasting greens and whites, from Dragonwell to Silver Needle, are great with spicy dishes, and brisk teas are divine with rich or hearty dishes. Experiment—it's fun!

For pairing teas with foods not made with tea, opt for a balance of fla-vors wherever possible. For example, a spicy Chinese meal works best with a rich, satisfying sweetish oolong or a very asserting green, like a Mao Feng green, a Ceylon green, or, again, Dragonwell.

Asian meals, in general, take well to a variety of lightly brewed greens. A light luncheon of a fruit salad works well with a fragrant tea like a Cameroon or a more delicate Darjeeling. A salad of mild greens dressed with a light milky or cheese-based dressing would be quite nice with a classic Keemun or brisk Ceylon black tea. (Salad dressings or other foods made with vinegar often conflict with tea.)

Pairing teas with traditional European cuisine like French or Italian can be quite an adventure in tasting. The choices we like with fish or poultry would be smooth blacks like Yunnan, Keemun, or the Nilgiris. Pastas, spicy tomato-based sauces, and rich cheese dishes work well with clean Ceylons such as Uva, Dimbula, or Kandy, and certainly Kenya is an ideal black tea for all meat meals or any hearty dish like a stew or chili.

For picnic fare or outdoor meals of any kind, nothing is quite as refreshing or as wonderful as an iced tea, and both black and green iced ver-sions are cooling and thirst-quenching. Creating iced teas takes no time at all, particularly if you make a "sun tea" style. Take a large, clean, gallon glass jar, put in 1 tea bag or 1 teaspoon/5 grams of black tea per 6 ounces/180 milliliters of spring water. Put the lid on tightly, and set the jar out on the porch or patio in the morning. By lunchtime, the kind sun will have brewed a soft, delicious tea for you. Add ice and serve. Once you taste sun tea, you'll never go back to bottled teas again. Green tea should be made just prior to serving. Brew with under-the-boil water, cooled further, then poured into glasses with just a little ice. To avoid diluting teas, use ice cubes made from fresh or even leftover juice or tea.

Generally, scented or fruited teas taste best with desserts or alone, for the delicacy of the fruit or scent can be lost among more assertive flavors in foods.

Obviously, taste being the subjective thing that it is, these suggestions are not meant to be definitive. Which teas are best suited to which foods is a decision your own palate has the privilege (and delight) of making.

Considering the variety of tea choices available in the marketplace, let your imagination run wild! Sample this and that, and rest assured that your palate can become sophisticated and knowledgeable if you are willing to taste widely. Most of the pleasure of cooking with tea, drinking tea, or pairing teas with foods is derived from what new taste experience may lie just around the corner.

To help in all the decision making, you can do tea tastings of type with type or type against type, such as sweet China greens with more assertive India greens, Darjeelings with Assams, or Ceylons with Africans. Or, switch and compare greens from Japan with blacks from Indonesia. No need to be agog or intimidated; have fun with tea.

SEASONAL MENUS

Now that you've tried cooking with tea, perhaps you'd like to present a menu composed of tea-infused foods. For suggestions, we have created one for every season, plus a holiday menu. Feel free to add crudités or salads, breads, or rice as desired. These are, as are all our suggestions, simply jumping-off points to fuel your own creativity, invitations to personalize the menu using some of your recipe favorites.

Spring

Springtime calls for foods of the season and a lighter menu. Start off with these appetizers, followed by a rich, aromatic fish with intoxicating mushrooms, and top it off with an elegant dessert.

Spring Rolls with Thai Tea Sauce

Sassy Bass with Aromatic Rub

Tea-Smoked Mushrooms

Chocolate Melting Moments Torte with Tea Crème Anglaise

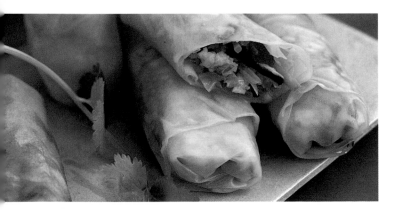

Choose from one of the many Thai iced tea mixes available for the appetizer, or make your own using a hearty black tea seasoned with star anise and vanilla. Great hot, too. For the entrée, choose an assertive Assam or pungent Pu-erh to stand up to the spices used in the rub. For dessert, consider a counterpoint in flavors: Iced Tea Lemonade with Lemon-Rosemary Sorbet or opt for a complementary hot Assam.

Summer

*Summertime is for coolness in the mouth and simple fare on the plate.
You can't go wrong with these choices; each has its own distinctive but
complementary flavors from tea infusions.*

Smoked Salmon Filets with Lapsang Souchong Cream Sauce

Cold Tea Noodles

Tea-Wilted Greens with Summer Fruit and Goat Cheese

Jasmine-Lemongrass Tea Sorbet

The obvious choice for the summer is the delightfully refreshing
Keemun-Kantaloupe Kooler, which is delicious anytime. However,
contrary though it may seem, hot tea is actually cooler on the
system than iced drinks. So bring out a pot of Lapsang Souchong
or a delicate Jasmine green and enjoy your tea and the summer
evening breeze.

Fall

Whether it's the leaves falling as they change colors or the promise of the holidays ahead, autumn means an increase in spices to warm the heart and the body. Here is a trio of hearty foods to get the season off to a great start. The menu shows a nice balance between the citrus and tang of the sauces and the warm strength of the marinades and smoking techniques for the entrées.

Tea "Smoked" Trout with Indian Salsa

Rata-tea-ouille

Broiled Tea-Glazed Oranges with Flan Thé

Hot Assam tea is the classic hot tea for a meal like this, but don't forget other hearty favorites like Kenya, Keemun, or any one of the wonderful blacks from Sri Lanka: Dimbula, Uva, or Kandy.

Winter

Ah, winter! The light is shorter, the need for warmth even greater. Bring on the stews and soups and, of course, the brisket! Ours is good enough to satisfy the biggest appetite, and the rice adds chewy goodness.

Brisket Braised in Tea with Root Vegetables

Red Rice in Oolong Tea

Awesome Assam Lemon Tart

Hot oolong tea is a treat; try the finest you can find, like a top-grade Formosa oolong, a Ti Kwan Yin. Or, you might opt for drinking black teas with a few drops of hot milk and honey to make the colder night seem more kind.

Holiday Dinner with Three Appetizers and Three Desserts

(That's why it's a HOLIDAY!)

Whatever you celebrate, do it with style, and a grand buffet. These selections are perfect for company because they're pretty, they're bountiful, and they say welcome to all appetites and tastes. And, YES, you must serve several desserts. How else to promise a sweet year for all?

Appetizers

Foie Gras with Tea-Infused Apricots

Jasmine-Cured Salmon with Lime-Mustard Sauce

Jade Shrimp in Lung Ching Tea

Entrée

Pork Tenderloin Cameroon with Prune-Stuffed Apples

Desserts

Earl Grey Truffles

Chai Ice Cream

Tea-Poached Plums

Because it's a holiday event, consider serving different teas with each course, as you would wines. Consider the crisp welcome of a Kenya with appetizers, the sweet smoothness of a dark black Cameroon to echo the sauce for an entrée cooked with Cameroon, and for dessert(s), offer a trio of choices: hot chai in clear glass mugs, a hot Earl Grey in lovely porcelain cups with the chocolates on the saucer, and a sweet Keemun in a mug along with a bowl of the plums. To end the evening—after the plates are cleared, the kitchen is cleaned up, and the guests have left—sit down alone or with your most special friends, bring out your prized Yixing pot and small thimble cups, and prepare a small serving of delicate Jasmine tea. Drink it as a cup of calm after a fabulous holiday event and to toast a world rich with friendship, good food, and the wonders of tea.

A Final Word…

Africa, China, Sri Lanka, India, Japan, Thailand, Vietnam, Taiwan—these are just a few stops around the world whose influence is reflected in our recipes. Each of these countries, plus the nearly 30 others that grow this remarkable leaf, has something unique in aroma, taste, body to offer you in your quest for the perfect cup to drink, the perfect brew to infuse your cooking. We hope we've tickled your curiosity, titillated your palate, tempted you to look at the tea shop with new eyes, and made you eager to try a new tea today. We wish you bon voyage around teadom and bon appétit *Cooking with Tea.*

Glossary of Words Used for Tea Tasting

We hope these definitions will guide you to develop your own vocabulary for tea. They are typical of the professional tea-taster's descriptions, but sometimes other words, especially those for wine tasting, are more suitable, like back-of-the-mouth feel or retro-nasal; full mouth feel; fruity or specific fruit such as grapey.

agony of the leaves. A dramatic term to indicate the unfurling of the leaves as they move up and down when hot water begins to infuse them.

aroma. The smell of the dry leaf, infused leaf, and the tea liquor itself; good ones are described as flowery or fruit-like. Both the dry and wet leaves have an aroma that is unique to the source of the tea, be it an area, such as Darjeeling, or an estate, such as Margaret's Hope.

astringency. A desired characteristic, particularly of Darjeelings, with a flavor characteristic described as a bite.

bakey. An undesirable characteristic usually resulting from firing the leaves at too high a temperature, which removes too much water too quickly. Not as bad as burnt, but not pleasant.

black. When a tea is fully 100% oxidized it becomes brownish black. The Chinese still call these teas reds because the infusions are various degrees of red.

body. A combination of the weight of the liquor on the tongue, the strength of the taste, and the full-mouth feel. Can be different degrees from light to full.

bright. Term to describe a tea leaf that appears shiny, a signal that there will be a brisk, lively taste in the cup; a taste that feels sparkling on the tongue, a desirable characteristic of most fine teas.

brisk. Term to describe a taste that is lively in the mouth, light yet pleasantly dry. Beautifully processed teas will have this desirable characteristic.

clean. Particularly important in cooking with tea; teas that are clean of stalks, dust, fibers, twigs or other bush, and leaf particles mean a cleaner taste in the recipe or the cup.

coppery. Bright tea leaves of a well-manufactured tea that have a reddish overcast.

creaming up. Considered harmless, this is an occasional bubbly residue that "comes up" to the surface of some black teas, especially Assams. Some attribute this to low-quality water, but that is not correct.

color. The color of infused tea is quite often misleading; sometimes a cup will look as pale as water yet have a strong taste; sometimes tea will be nearly black but lack any pungency in either aroma or taste. Color, then, is unrelated to taste. Brew by quantity and the clock, not by color!

flat. Not a good quality, indicating age or at least a lack of freshness; can also result from poor storage.

fruity. A wonderful quality of fine oolongs, almost indescribable in its satiny taste on the tongue and exquisite aroma. Mainland China Keemuns and Yunnans can have this, too, as do black Cameroons.

gone off. Tea that is stale or bad smelling; run, don't walk, when confronted with a tea whose flavor and aroma have "gone off" to tea hell.

malty. Frequently attributed to Assams, this flavor characteristic is slightly smoky, rich, with a full-mouth feel. Not as frequently found in modern processed Assams, but still a highly desirable characteristic.

muscatel. A classic flavor characteristic of Darjeeling teas; a winey taste; most desirable. It is also a particular plucking, done with stunted leaves from the first shoots of the second plucking, yielding a very small harvest usually available from the end of May to the first weeks of June.

musty. Moldy taste or smell that results from poor packing or storage. Not to be confused with the desirable musty smell of Pu-erhs, which are intentionally aged with a friendly mold or bacteria.

nose. The smell of the dried tea leaf; can be good or bad. Let your "nose" be your guide.

peak. This is that magical moment when body, flavor, astringency, and aroma converge in the mouth for an ecstatic moment. It is the holy grail moment of tea tasting and more often attributed to black teas than greens or oolongs.

self-drinking. A tea perfect by itself with no need to blend, flavor, or add lemon, milk, or sugar, because it has an ideal combination of flavor, body, color, and aroma—the four elements of a perfect tea.

stewed. Leaves that have been overbrewed or "stewed" will become bitter. Sometimes leaves fired poorly will result in a bitter taste no matter how well they have been brewed. You can sometimes make a decent cup from so-so tea, but nothing will help poorly made tea.

sweet. The word sweet does not ever mean there is sugar mixed in the tea leaf; it means it has a soft, sweetish taste in the same way that butter lettuce is sweeter than chard.

tarry. Describes the aroma that results from teas such as Lapsang Souchong or Russian Caravan blends that are smoked over charcoal or various woods.

tip. An indicator of good picking, it is the pointed edge of the youngest leaves, usually white or silvery or coppery or golden. A leaf that is "tippy" usually indicates good flavor in the cup.

well-twisted. Tightly rolled, usually whole leaf teas of either oolong or black processed teas. The twisting is lengthwise and when opened, the leaves are large and, hopefully, full of flavor.

winey. A desirable flavor characteristic that results in a mellow, rich taste like Chinese Keemuns.

Resources for Unusual Ingredients

While every effort has been made to use ingredients available in the ethnic departments of major grocery stores or at the growing numbers of ethnic grocers popping up everywhere, some ingredients may be harder to find than others.

Some ingredients are available fresh or canned, such as lychee; others should definitely only be used fresh, such as lemongrass. Others, like ginger root, should be bought fresh and cut for each use. Do not use ground ginger in our recipes, unless directed.

Bakery products like lavash, kataifi, and eggroll wrappers are available at many major supermarkets in the ethnic food sections, or seek them out at specialty markets near you.

All of the following sources offer free catalogs or inventory lists. Buy in small quantities and use them quickly for best results. Spices, in particular, should be purchased in small quantities and ground fresh as you need them. Preground spices fade quickly in both color and flavor. Whenever possible, choose an ethnic market close to you as a primary choice, where the supply is constant and consistently fresh and the turnover of inventory is quick.

Adriana's Caravan
409 Vanderbilt Street
Brooklyn, NY 11218
(800) 316-0820
Fax: (718) 436-8565
e-mail: Adriana@aol.com
*Free mail order catalog of more than 1,500
spices, condiments, and exotic ingredients from
around the world.*

Aphrodisia
264 Bleecker Street
New York, NY 10014
(212) 989-6440
Fax: (212) 989-8027
Mail order available

Atlantic Spice Co.
P.O. Box 205
North Truro, MA 02652
(800) 316-7965 or (508) 487-6100
Fax: (508) 487-2550
www.atlanticspice.com
Free catalog of spices and teas

Chocolates El Rey, Inc.
P.O. Box 853
Fredericksburg, TX 78624
(800) ELREY-99 or 357-3999
www.chocolate-elrey.com
Excellent Venezuela chocolate for baking;
available on-line or at Whole Foods, Dean & DeLuca,
and Fresh Fields.

Chocovic Chocolates of Spain
www.chocovic.com
Offers a full range of chocolates at varying degrees of
cocoa butter content. Jade, their dark milk chocolate
variety, goes beautifully with a cup of creamy Assam tea.
Ocumare, a bittersweet version, adds layers and richness
to a frothy blend of sweetly spiced black tea and milk for
a winter mug.

Cluizel Chocolates
Paris, France
(800) 207-7058 or (323) 581-7999 x107
Sells fine Venezuelan chocolate, much of which is
comprised of single varietal cocoa beans. A standout
among standouts, the dark milk chocolate is for chocoholics
only. Chocolate of consistent taste and texture and worth
its somewhat high price. Ask for local sources.

Colusari® Red Rice
Indian Harvest Specialtifoods, Inc.
P.O. Box 428
Bemidji, MN 56619-0428
(800) 346-7032
www.indianharvest.com
Superior source for unique and unusual rice and
grain products.

Frontier Cooperative Herbs
P.O. Box 299
Norway, IA 53218
(800) 669-3275
www.frontiercoop.com
e-mail:peggy.amans@frontiercoop.com
Extensive free catalog of herbs and spices.

Kalustyan
123 Lexington Avenue
New York, NY 10016
(212) 685-3451
International grocer with good choices of spices.

Nature's Herbs
47444 Kato Street
Fremont, CA 94538
(510) 651-4591
Free catalog of extensive list of spices and herbs.

Penzeys, Ltd.
P.O. Box 923
Muskego, WI 53150
(414) 574-0277
www.penzeys.com
A family-owned spice firm that offers a staggering array of whole spices and custom blends.

Rafal Spice Company
2521 Russell Street
Detroit, MI 48207
(800) 228-4276 or (313) 259-6373
Fresh spices and spice blends are a specialty. Free catalog.

Royal Pacific Foods (dba The Ginger People)
2700 Garden Road Suite G
Monterey, CA 93940
(800) 551-5284 or (831) 645-1090
info@gingerpeople.com
Purveyors of fine ginger products, including fresh ginger juice.

San Francisco Herb Co.
250 Fourteenth Street
San Francisco, CA 94103
(800) 227-4530 or (415) 861-7174
Fax: (415) 861-4440
www.sfherb.com
Excellent sources of both whole and powdered spices.

Resources for Connoisseur Teas and Teapots

Although there are hundreds more places to buy teas and accessories, this list reflects companies that are known for consistently selling high-quality, loose-leaf teas in the United States.

Adagio Teas
40-10 Kuiken Terrace
Fair Lawn, NJ 07410
(877) ADAGIO-T
www.discovertea.com
Limited but carefully chosen selection of teas, accessories, and teapots. Individual tea cups with infusers are neat.

Algabar
920 North La Cienega Boulevard
Los Angeles, CA 90069
(310) 360-3500
This home accessories shop has wonderful tabletop tea ware and selections from the French line of teas, Mariage Frères.

Barnes & Watson Fine Teas
1319 Dexter Avenue North
Suite 30
Seattle, WA 98109
(206) 283-6948
Fax: (206) 283-0799
www.barnesandwatson.com
Excellent line of fine teas wholesaled to fine restaurants, hotels, and chefs.

Bengal Bay
www.bengalbay.com
Over 250 teas from all categories.

Chado Tea Room
8422 $\frac{1}{2}$ West Third Street
Los Angeles, CA 90048
(323) 655-2056
Lovely tea room and tea shop featuring high-end tea selections and unique tea accessories, including the Tea-One. Mail order available.

Choice Organic Teas, Granum, Inc.
2901 NE Blakely Street
Seattle, WA 98105
(206) 525-0051
Fax: (206) 523-9750
One of the pioneers in packaged organic teas, Choice has increased its selection and upgraded its quality every year. Available at most upscale and health-food stores.

Corti Brothers
5810 Folsom Boulevard
P.O. Box 191358
Sacramento, CA 95819
(916) 736-3800
Fax: (916) 736-3807
Upscale market for spices and exquisite, exclusive

Chinese teas chosen by a wine connoisseur with an equally sophisticated palate for tea. Mail order available. Ask for their newsletter.

East India Tea and Coffee Co., Ltd.
1933 Davis Street
Suite 308
San Leandro, CA 94577
(510) 638-1300
Fax: (510) 638-0760
Garden Estate Teas in nicely designed packages.

Golden Moon Tea, Ltd.
P.O. Box 1646
Woodinville, WA 98072
(425) 576-0179
Fax: (425) 576-0410
One of the premier packaged lines of tea, each selected for its high quality, superb taste, and rarity. Limited reserve teas. Mail order and at upscale markets everywhere.

Grace Tea Company, Ltd., New York
50 West 17th Street
New York, NY 10011
(212) 255-2935
Winey Keemun and Before the Rain Jasmine are benchmark teas of this limited but very impressive inventory of quality teas, elegantly packaged in their signature black tins. Mail order list.

Guy's Tea/Empire Tea Services
5155 Hartford Avenue
Columbus, IN 47203
(812) 375-1937
Fax: (812) 376-7382
e-mail: CeylonTea@Juno.com
www.guystea.com
Fine selections of teas from Sri Lanka including a 100-percent Ceylon green.

Harney & Sons
11 East Main Street
Village Green
P.O. Box 638
Salisbury, CT 06068
(888) HARNEY T (427-6398)
Fax: (203) 435-5044
www.harney.com
Good line of classic teas, organics, greens, and many rare and specialized teas, available from the Web site or through their elegant mail order catalog.

Himalayan Highland Tea Company
1702 South Hwy. 121
Suite 607-189
Lewisville, TX 75067
(800) 580-8585
Fax: (972) 221-6770
Importers of a variety of teas from Nepal.

Holy Mountain Trading Co.
P.O. Box 457
Fairfax, CA 94978
(888) 832-8008
www.holymtn.com
Fine teas and extensive collection of Yixing ware and a terrific Web site.

The Honorable Jane Company
10209 Main Street
Potter Valley, CA 95469
(888) 743-1966
e-mail: dearjane@honorablejane.com
www.honorablejane.com
Fine teas and accessories, chosen with care and a good eye for style; mail order from their utterly charming catalog.

The House of Tea, Ltd.
720 South Fourth Street
Philadelphia, PA 19147
(215) 923-8327
Fax: (215) 923-6121
www.houseoftea.com
Carefully created collection of fine teas offered in the shop or order by mail.

Imperial Tea Court
1411 Powell Street
San Francisco, CA 94133
(415) 788-6080 or (800) 567-5898
Fax: (415) 788-6079
www.imperialtea.com
e-mail: imperial@imperialtea.com
Since 1995, this authentic Chinese tea room has become the place for sampling and buying fine Chinese teas. All teas and accessories available by mail order.

The Indochina Tea Co.
P.O. Box 1032
Studio City, CA 91614-0032
(323) 650-8020
Fax: (323) 650-8022
Exclusive importers of premium teas from Vietnam, each with a provocative story and unique taste.

Justin Lloyd Premium Tea Co.
1111 Watson Center Road Unit A-1
Carson, CA 90745
(310) 834-4400, ext. 5 or (800) 962-6331
Chinese-style, brilliant red and black "lacquer" tins house an excellent line of loose-leaf teas and blends. Tea bag line also. At fine food shops everywhere.

le T Fine Tea Trading Company
Route de Begnins 6
CH-1196 Gland, Switzerland
Tel: 011-41 (0)22 995 14 00
Fax: 011-41 (0)22 995 14 03
http://www.le-t.com
denis.braunschweig@le-t.com
Limited but well-chosen inventory of teas plus some excellent accessories for the discriminating tea lover.

Leaves Pure Leaves
1392 Lowrie Avenue
San Francisco, CA 94080
(650) 583-1157
Fax: (650) 583-1163
www.leaves.com
e-mail: Pureteas@leaves.com
The clean design of the package is just the first sign of quality in this excellent packaged line of high-end, loose-leaf teas. Available at fine shops everywhere or on-line.

Lindsay's Teas
380 Swift Avenue
Suite 10
South San Francisco, CA 94080
(650) 952-5446
Fax: (650) 871-4845
Carefully blended line of good-quality teas comes in round colorful canisters that are great for gift giving and solo sipping. New organic lines.

Mariage Frères (See Algabar)
www.mariagefreres.com
e-mail: postmaster@mariagefreres.com

Mark T. Wendell, Importer
P.O. Box 1312
West Concord, MA 01742
(978) 369-3709
Fax: (978) 369-7992
People either love or hate Hu-Kwa, the strong, earthy Lapsang Souchong-style tea that made this company famous. Vivid choice for smoking foods with tea.

The Peaceful Dragon Tea House and Cultural Center
McMullen Creek Market
8324-509 Pineville-Matthews Rd.
Charlotte, NC 28226
(704) 544-1012
Fax: (704) 544-7015
www.peacefuldragon.com
Have a complete Oriental cultural experience: Chinese teas in Yixing pots, Japanese teas in black ironstone, or take a class in Tai Chi before or after tea. All teas and accessories available by mail order.

Peet's Coffee & Tea
P.O. Box 12509
Berkeley, CA 94712
(800) 999-2132 ext. 220
Fax: (510) 704-0311
Tea merchants since 1966, Peet's teas include a constantly changing group of "rare teas," which are always worth the sip. Available at over twenty-five stores in northern California and by mail order.

Perennial Tea Room
1910 Ophally
Seattle, WA 98101
(888) 448-4054 or
(206) 448-4054
70+ tea selections and huge selection of tea pots. Mail order accepted.

Red Crane Teas
2351 Federal Boulevard #405
Denver, CO 80211
(303) 477-3642
www.redcraneteas.com
e-mail:sk@redcraneteas.com
Carefully selected, limited inventory of teas that are the highest quality. Available by mail order.

The Republic of Tea
8 Digital Drive
Suite 100
Novato, CA 94949
(800) 298-4TEA
fax: (618) 478-2116
www.republicoftea.com

Interesting organic line; extensive line of green teas plus their classic traditional teas with charming names and pretty packages. Available at fine shops and from their free, fun-to-browse catalog.

Robert & Joseph, Ltd.
6281 Martin Lane
Red Granite, WI 54970-9533
(414) 566-2520 or (414) 566-2275
Limited selection of high-quality teas available by mail order.

Royal Gardens Tea Company
P.O. Box 2390
Fort Bragg, CA 95437
(707) 961-0263
www.thanksgivingcoffee.com
Limited but well-chosen teas in beautiful packages, available in upscale markets or call for their catalog.

serendipitea
P.O. Box 81
Ridgefield, CT 06877
(888) TEA LIFE (832-5433)
Fax: (203) 894-9649
www.serendipitea.com
Excellent, limited selection of prime teas, clever accessories, and great soap made with tea. Mail order catalog by request.

Silk Road Teas
P.O. Box 287
Lagunitas, CA 94938
(415) 488-9017
Fax: (415) 488-9015

David Lee Hoffman doesn't just sell tea, he grows it. He encourages the efforts of the Chinese organic tea farmer, and his teas never disappoint. The selection is fabulous, artfully and respectfully packaged, and worth every penny. Mail order list.

Simpson & Vail Inc., Quality Teas & Coffees Since 1929
3 Quarry Rd.
Brookfield, CT 06804
(800) 282-TEAS
www.svtea.com
More than 120 tea selections plus accessories from around the world. Buy on-line, mail order through their extensive print catalog, or give them a call.

Sinotique
19A Mott Street
New York, NY 10013
(212) 587-2393
Classes in gung fu; superior selections of teas.

Societe du Thé
2708 Lyndale Avenue South
Minneapolis, MN 55408
(888) 871-5148
Fax: (612) 874-0239
www.la-societe-du-the.com
Shop for fine teas from around the world via mail order, on-line, or at its premises.

SpecialTeas, Inc.
2 Reynolds Street
Norwalk, CT 06855
(888) 365-6983
Fax: (203) 975-4566

www.specialteas.com
For the connoisseur, this is a serious, dedicated source for superior teas.

Stash Teas
P.O. Box 910
Portland, OR 97207
(800) 547-1514
Fax: (503) 684-1514
www.stashtea.com
Stash has everything for the tea lover from unique pots to both bulk and packaged teas. New organic line.

Tao of Tea
3430 SE Belmont St.
Portland, OR 97214
(503) 736-0119
www.taooftea.com
Open daily for sampling extremely rare teas and the classics, all served in the appropriate vessels. Specialties include whisked hot or iced matcha. Yixing pots, accessories, and teas available by mail order.

Tazo
P.O. Box 66
Portland, OR 97207
(503) 231-9234
Fax: (503) 231-8801
Incredible packaging matched by quality teas, including refreshing greens made with pure botanicals, has caught the eye of discerning tea lovers everywhere. Starbucks now offers Tazo exclusively at all its locations.

Tea & Company
2207 Fillmore Street

San Francisco, CA 94115
(415) 929-TEAS
Clean light woods, high ceilings, comfortable seating, all are part of this hip tea spot in one of the most delightful areas of the city. Great teas and nice accessories. Mail order accepted.

The Teacup
2207 Queen Avenue North
Seattle, WA 98109
(206) 283-5931
Fax: (206) 284-6784
Very respectable inventory of fine teas and lovely accessories. Mail order.

TeaRex
2102 South Blvd. #150
Charlotte, NC 28203-5004
(704) 371-4440
www.tearex.com
100+ varieties personally cupped by the owner. Antique and contemporary tea accessories.

TeaSource
752 Cleveland Avenue South
(Highland Park)
St. Paul, MN 55116
(651) 690-9822
Exceptional tea shop with 200+ selections of well-chosen teas aimed at the sophisticated palate.

The Tea House, Purveyors of Fine Teas and Accessories
541 Fessler Avenue
Naperville, IL 62565
(630) 961-0877

Fax: (630) 961-0817

www.theteahouse.com

Excellent line of primarily Chinese teas plus superb selections of flavored teas.

Teaism, A Tea House

2009 R Street NW

Washington, DC 20009

(888) 8-TEAISM or (202) 667-3827

Now with three locations, this innovative restaurant has an in-depth menu of foods infused with tea, plus a great selection for drinking or to take home. Mail order available for teas. Other locations are in Lafayette Park, 800 Connecticut Avenue, NW, Washington, DC 20005 (202) 835-2233, open weekdays only, and 400 Eighth Street, NW, Washington, DC 20003, (202) 667-3827, open daily. All serve the same fine teas and similar menus but hours vary.

Tealuxe

Zero Brattle Street

Harvard Square

Cambridge, MA 02138

(617) 441-0077

www.tealuxe.com

A great tea bar right off Harvard Square to enjoy superb teas all day, every day. Teas sold by the gram. An excellent list of teas, brewed by the clock and with great care. Extensive list of other fine teas and accessories for take-away, on-line or mail order.

Tearoom T

1568 West Broadway

Vancouver, BC V6J5K9

Canada

(604) 874-8320

Fax: (604) 261-5060

www.tealeaves.com

A gathering of the finest estate teas of the world presented by a corps of young devotees who truly understand what the tea experience is all about.

Tea Time

542 Ramona Street

Palo Alto, CA 94301

(650) 328-2877

or (800) 877-2877

www.tea-time.com

Thoughtfully selected inventory of fine teas and accessories available in their fun shop or on their Web site.

Ten Ren Tea and Ginseng Co., Inc.

50 Mott Street

New York, NY 10013

(800) 292-2049 (212) 349-2286

Fax: (212) 349-2180

and

135-18 Roosevelt Avenue

Flushing NY 11354

(718) 461-9305

Also in Monterey Park and San Francisco, California, and in Chicago, Illinois. Superb Formosa teas and other fine loose-leaf teas and accessories.

Thompson's Fine Teas

2062 South Delaware

San Mateo, CA 94403

(800) 830-8835
Fax: (650) 572-9857
e-mail: Info@fineteas.com
www.fineteas.com
Limited but very selective inventory of fine teas and accessories, including some from Vietnam.

Todd & Holland Tea Merchants
7577 Lake Street
River Forest, IL 60305
(800) 747-8327
Fax: (708) 488-1246
www.todd-holland.com
Very fine inventory of fine teas. Store is as elegant and stylish as its teas and accessories. Catalog and newsletter available.

Upton Tea Imports
231 South Street
Hopkinton, MA 01748
(800) 234-TEAS
www.upton.com
Since 1989, Tom Eck has sold exemplary teas from his extensive catalog, which presently lists more than 200 teas available by mail order or on-line.

Water & Leaves Company
690 Broadway
Redwood City, CA 94063
(800) 699-4753
Fax: (650) 363-0847
www.wayoftea.com
Elegantly packaged, fine Chinese teas, particularly greens and oolongs; Yixing pots. Mail order and in fine markets everywhere.

Windham Tea Club
12 Wilson Road
Windham, NH 03087
(800) 565-7527
Informative membership newsletter highlights their carefully selected teas and strong commitment to tea education. Ask about their tea of the month program.

World Treasure Trading Co.
815 Piner Road
Santa Rosa, CA 95403
(707) 566-7888
Fax: (707) 566-7890
Long-time importer of Yixing teaware of both elegant and whimsical designs. Available at fine houseware and tea shops everywhere.

Photo Credits

Unless otherwise indicated, all photo styling was performed by Susan Bourgoin. All teas shown in the photos are from India Tea Importers of Montebello, California, and Chado Tea Room of Los Angeles. All accessories are from the collections of the authors or the photographer, except those noted below.

p. 18, tea chart: teas courtesy of India Tea Importers. The teas are: 1. Lapsang Souchong; 2. Earl Grey; 3. Keemun; 4. Cameroon; 5. Assam; 6. Kenya; 7. Darjeeling; 8. Genmaicha; 9. Silver Needle; 10. Nepal; 11. Red Mudan; 12. Green Mudan; 13. Jasmine Yin Hao; 14. Yunnan.

p. 30, technique shot, aromatic rub: blue plate from the collection of Mr. Kittibhoom Harnpatanakitpanich

p. 71 Pork Tenderloin Cameroon with Prune-Stuffed Apples: aqua Cyclamen plate courtesy of Freehand

p. 72, Sassy Bass with Aromatic Rub: yellow Cyclamen dish courtesy of Freehand

p. 75, Smoked Salmon Filets with Lapsang Souchong Cream Sauce: plate courtesy of Freehand

p. 81, Tea-Sauced Scallops with Orange, Soy, and Honey: styling by Kathleen Biernat

p. 83 Tea-Smoked Chicken Wraps: yellow glazed plate courtesy of Freehand

p. 85, Tea "Smoked" Trout with Indian Salsa: celadon accessories from the collection of Mr. Kittibhoom Harnpatanakitpanich

p. 102, Green Tea-Poached Asian Pears with Pistachio Cream Sauce: styling by Kathleen Biernat

p. 111, Peaches in Kenya Tea Sauce: Sonnegard white bowl and celadon plates courtesy of Algabar

p. 113, Real Green Tea Ice Cream: dark teal ripple plate courtesy of Freehand

p. 116, Keemun–Kantaloupe Kooler, Iced Tea Lemonade with Lemon–Rosemary Sorbet, Iced Tea with Lemongrass Syrup: table courtesy of Freehand

Sources for Accessories

Algabar, 920 La Cienega Boulevard, Los Angeles, CA 90069, (310) 360-3500, Gail Baral, owner
Chado Tea Room, 8422 1/2 West Third Street, Los Angeles, CA 90048, (323) 655-2056, Devan and Reena Shah, owners
Freehand, 8413 West Third Street, Los Angeles, CA 90048, (323) 655-2607, Carol Sauvion, owner
India Tea Importers, 1629 Date Street, Montebello, CA 90640 (323) 722-9438, Devan Shah, owner